"In those days, when your numbers have increased greatly in the land," declares the Lord, "people will no longer say, 'The ark of the covenant of the Lord.' It will never enter their minds or be remembered; it will not be missed, nor will another one be made."

—Jeremiah 3:16 (NIV)

MYSTERIES & WONDERS of the BIBLE

Unveiled: Tamar's Story
A Life Renewed: Shoshan's Story
Garden of Secrets: Adah's Story
Among the Giants: Achsah's Story
Seeking Leviathan: Milkah's Story
A Flame of Hope: Abital's Story
Covenant of the Heart: Odelia's Story

MYSTERIES & WONDERS of the BIBLE

COVENANT OF THE HEART

ODELIA'S STORY

Heidi Chiavaroli

Guideposts

A Gift from Guideposts

Thank you for your purchase! We want to express our gratitude for your support with a special gift just for you.

Dive into **Spirit Lifters**, a complimentary e-book that will fortify your faith, offering solace during challenging moments. Its 31 carefully selected scripture verses will soothe and uplift your soul.

Please use the QR code or go to **guideposts.org/spiritlifters** to download.

Mysteries & Wonders of the Bible is a trademark of Guideposts.

Published by Guideposts
100 Reserve Road, Suite E200, Danbury, CT 06810
Guideposts.org

Copyright © 2025 by Guideposts. All rights reserved. This book, or parts thereof, may not be reproduced, stored in a retrieval system, or transmitted in any form or by any means, electronic, mechanical, photocopying, recording, or otherwise, without the written permission of the publisher.

This is a work of fiction. While the characters and settings are drawn from scripture references and historical accounts, apart from the actual people, events, and locales that figure into the fiction narrative, all other names, characters, places, and events are the creation of the author's imagination or are used fictitiously. Every attempt has been made to credit the sources of copyrighted material used in this book. If any such acknowledgment has been inadvertently omitted or miscredited, receipt of such information would be appreciated.

Scripture references are from the following sources: *The Holy Bible, King James Version* (KJV). *The Holy Bible, New International Version* (NIV). Copyright © 1973, 1978, 1984, 2011 by Biblica, Inc. Used by permission of Zondervan. All rights reserved worldwide. www.zondervan.com.

Cover and interior design by Müllerhaus
Cover illustration by Brian Call represented by Illustration Online LLC.
Typeset by Aptara, Inc.

ISBN 978-1-961251-86-1 (hardcover)
ISBN 978-1-961251-87-8 (softcover)
ISBN 978-1-961251-88-5 (epub)

Printed and bound in the United States of America
10 9 8 7 6 5 4 3 2 1

MYSTERIES & WONDERS of the BIBLE

COVENANT OF THE HEART

ODELIA'S STORY

CAST OF CHARACTERS

Biblical Characters

Baruch • scribe and friend of the prophet Jeremiah

Gedaliah • Shaphan's grandson, placed in charge as governor to those remaining in Judah after the Babylonian captivity

Gemariah • temple priest and son of Shaphan

Ishmael • member of the royal household of Judah who resented Gedaliah being appointed governor over the Jewish people after the Babylonian captivity

Jeremiah • priest who prophesied God's impending judgment. His ministry was from around 626 BC until after 586 BC.

Johanan • leader who rallied around Gedaliah after he was appointed governor

King Zedekiah • final king of Judah before the Babylonian conquest

Pashhur • priest in charge of the temple who had Jeremiah beaten after he prophesied that Jerusalem would be destroyed

Seraiah • brother of Baruch and officer of King Zedekiah. Likely a follower of Jeremiah.

Shaphan • temple secretary who brought the Book of the Law to King Josiah.

Fictional Characters

Aden • adopted son of Baruch and priest-in-training

Adino • woodworker who drinks too much whom Odelia's parents wish her to marry

Avigail • cousin of Odelia

Eliana • wife of one of the priests

Eliashib • elder priest in charge of the group leaving Jerusalem

Hashem • Ammonite orphan boy left at Jerusalem's city walls when he became sick

Jehoahaz • commanding soldier of the group that leaves Jerusalem with the ark

Odelia • daughter of Pashhur

Sherah • childhood friend of Odelia's and sister of Jehoahaz

Tiamet • Babylonian commander

Zillah • friend of Sherah who is betrothed to Jehoahaz. She also serves as the group's midwife and healer.

GLOSSARY OF TERMS

abba • father

Adonai • name for God considered acceptable to say aloud. Meaning "Lord" or "Master."

Adonai El Elyon • name for God meaning "The Lord Most High God"

ahuvati • beloved

bet • house

El Shaddai • name for God meaning "Almighty"

emmer • an ancient wheat, also known as farro

hesed • faithful, loving commitment of God to His people

imma • mother

kinsman redeemer • a relative who, according to the Law, would act on behalf of his kin to deliver or rescue them from debt or trouble. Often the brother of an Israelite who died would act as a redeemer by marrying his brother's wife and providing a son for his deceased brother.

kuphar • round boat used on the Tigris and Euphrates rivers

mikveh • bath in which Hebrew cleansing rituals were performed

miter • head covering worn by the high priest when he served in the temple or tabernacle

mohar • price paid by the father of the groom to the father of the bride

savta • grandmother

Shekinah • the presence of God, usually used to refer to His dwelling place

shema • "to hear." Also a daily prayer spoken by ancient Israelites and still said by many today.

Tammuz • the fourth month on the Hebrew calendar, beginning the season of summer

teraphim • small household god

tzitzit • specially knotted prayer tassels worn on the garments of males as a reminder of God's commandments

Yahweh • name for God stemming from the Hebrew word "I AM." Often thought to be too holy to say.

CHAPTER ONE

The Ninth Year of King Zedekiah's Reign

Odelia gasped and sat up in bed, her breaths cinching tight in her chest. She clasped at the linen fabric of her night tunic, waiting for her heart to steady.

The dream. Again. Would the vision of the shattered clay jar and the words that accompanied them ever cease to haunt her?

She threw aside the quilt that twisted around her legs and pushed herself off the straw mattress. Air. She needed air.

Not bothering to slip on her sandals, she allowed her bare feet to slide along the smooth stone floor of their home. Her *abba*'s snores echoed outside her parents' bedchamber. Not until she entered the cobbled courtyard with its palm tree and limestone bench and climbed the stairs to the roof did she allow herself a full, satisfying breath.

She tilted her face to the twinkling stars above. As always, she remembered the story of *Adonai* instructing Abram to look to the heavens and count the stars, of the Lord's promise that his offspring would be as bountiful as the shimmering lights, that He would give them the land of Canaan.

This land. Odelia's homeland, now threatened by famine. Now threatened by King Nebuchadnezzar's army.

She inhaled a quivering breath. It was more comforting to meditate on the ancient promise rather than the promise in her dream that accompanied the shattered jar. Even now, the prophet Jeremiah's words sliced through the clear night and pierced her mind. Though she hadn't been older than four, Odelia would never forget them.

"I am going to bring on this city and all the villages around it every disaster I pronounced against them, because they were stiff-necked and would not listen to my words."

She shivered. What was wrong with her that she could not forget the words as easily as her abba had? As her aunts and uncles and friends? Was it the sight that followed the words? The fact that her abba, Pashhur, the priest in charge of the temple, had ordered Jeremiah whipped and put in the stocks for his emboldened claim? Or perhaps it was the name the prophet bequeathed to her abba: *Magor-Missabib.* Terror on Every Side.

Would the Lord enact His justice on Odelia simply for who her abba was? Would Adonai break her and her people beyond repair, as Jeremiah had broken that clay jar?

She rubbed her bare arms against the chill of the night air. Abba had cast off Jeremiah's words as ludicrous treason. But now, sixteen years since Jeremiah smashed the jar before the leaders and priests in the valley of Ben Hinnom, it appeared his words would finally come to pass.

The pungent, familiar scent of incense met her nostrils, and Odelia looked behind her to the rooftop adjacent to their *bet*. In the moonlight, a shadowy female figure in filmy garments and copper bangles on her ankles danced seductively around a small altar, waving the incense toward her as she moved. Odelia's face burned.

Avigail.

Perhaps Odelia could slip back into the walled courtyard below without her cousin's notice. She ducked down and with poise akin to that of a water buffalo, attempted to shimmy across the stone roof.

"Odelia!" A loud whisper came from the direction of the incense.

Odelia squeezed her eyes shut. She supposed it neither neighborly nor familial to ignore her cousin.

"Shalom, Avigail." She stifled a yawn, hoping her kinswoman would allow her to pass without conversation. But her cousin had never been one to be dissuaded, pressing Odelia into adventures outside the area of her comfort since they were small children. She gestured Odelia over. Sighing, Odelia made the short jump to the adjacent rooftop.

Avigail greeted her with a kiss on the cheek. "Shalom, cousin. It has been too long. How do we live so close and yet never see each other?"

Even in the dim light of the moon, Avigail's face glowed. Without the covering of a veil, her beautiful brown curls cascaded over her shoulders, framing high cheekbones and wide, kohl-lined eyes. If Odelia were half as pretty as her younger cousin, she would be married by now, starting her own family.

"*Imma* has suffered aches in her head of late. I have stayed close to help her." Though what Imma truly needed—water—was something all lacked the past few months. A drought had wilted the plants and leeched the soil of moisture. Their city was blocked by Nebuchadnezzar's army from receiving imports. People wailed at King Zedekiah's gates, begging him to do something. Others turned to their gods.

"Has she burned incense to the queen of heaven for healing? I am sure she will answer her. Join me now, Odelia, on behalf of your imma."

Odelia's gaze fell on the smoking incense, the rich scent of myrrh strong in the air. Beside it lay a small cake marked with the queen's image, and beside that, something wet. Odelia's stomach churned. She prayed to Adonai that her cousin did not waste precious water on the queen of heaven. "I am tired. I think I will return to bed."

Avigail squeezed Odelia's hands. "Come now, Odelia. You are far too serious for your own good. I am beseeching her for love and fertility, both of which I will soon find. You would do well to join me. You are not getting any younger, you know."

Odelia wrinkled her nose. "Thank you for that reminder, sweet cousin." And what good were love and fertility if everything they had was to be taken away by the Babylonians?

Avigail smiled. "I do not mean harm. Remember our adventures as children? How we followed the tunnels until our lamps threatened to burn out? You used to be so exciting, Odelia. What happened to that girl I once knew?"

What happened? Their land had been pillaged by the Babylonians, many of Odelia's friends taken captive in her tenth year. And now, the Babylonians returned, building siege ramps outside Jerusalem's walls. It would happen all over again. Perhaps even worse this time.

"I am going to bring on this city and all the villages around it every disaster I pronounced against them."

Odelia blinked and the image of Jeremiah's broken jar was replaced by Avigail's cake offering to the queen of heaven.

Avigail ignored Odelia's silence, wrapping fingers with hennaed nails around Odelia's wrist and pulling her closer to the small altar. "I had a prophecy from the Lord at the Asherah pole today."

"A prophecy from the Lord at an Asherah pole? Avigail—"

Odelia's cousin shook her head. "The Lord will bless me, I am certain of it."

Odelia sighed. She could hardly keep up with Avigail's many gods. That she threw in the One True God with all the others made Odelia's head spin. And yet, it was not uncommon to worship all the gods. On any given night, Odelia could look out upon the rooftops of Jerusalem and see the people burning incense to Baal or the queen of heaven. Her own imma, wife to a temple priest, had been known to participate in such activities.

Avigail tugged Odelia toward the burning incense. Something warm and wet dropped onto Odelia's hand. She turned Avigail's forearm over. "Cousin, what—" But the dark crimson stripes of blood on Avigail's flawless skin stopped her words. That wasn't a liquid offering of wine or water on Avigail's stone rooftop, but one of…blood.

Avigail avoided Odelia's gaze. "Sometimes the gods fall asleep. We must spill blood to wake them."

Odelia shook her head, the sight of her cousin's slashed and bloodied arm spinning in her mind alongside that of Jeremiah's shattered jar. Fury welled inside her. "Avigail, listen to yourself. What kind of god needs you—a mere mortal—to wake them up? What kind of power can they hold if they are so apt to fall asleep?"

Avigail snatched her arm from Odelia. "Do not judge me, cousin. All the gods—even Adonai—require sacrifice, do they not? The greater the sacrifice, the greater the reward."

She was right, of course. Gooseflesh broke out on Odelia's skin. Her next words came forth careful, measured. "Please tell me you have never been involved in the sacrifices of children at Topheth." Sacrifices in the very valley where Jeremiah had thrown his clay jar before her abba and the other priests and elders.

Avigail crossed her arms in front of her chest. "Fine. I will not tell you."

A muted groan of agony passed Odelia's lips. "Avigail, it is abominable. Jeremiah warned—"

"Who is to say Jeremiah is a true prophet?"

"Even if he were not... The killing of innocent youth, cousin?" She had heard stories of children being made to gather the very wood from which their abbas built sacrificial fires to offer their offspring.

"I did not invite you onto my rooftop to judge my beliefs. You have always thought yourself better than me, have you not, Odelia? But now, let us see who is to marry first and bear sons."

"What will any of it matter if our sons are dead by the hand of Nebuchadnezzar?"

"We have the temple with us. We are protected."

Odelia bit her lip. According to Jeremiah, Adonai grew impatient with His people—people who put their faith in His temple instead of Yahweh Himself.

Tentatively, she reached out a hand to her cousin. "I care for you, Avigail. That is why I show concern. Not because I think myself better than you. I know I am not." Had not Odelia's abba been responsible for the whipping and discipline of a man of God? How many times had Odelia seen the pagan worship of those around her and kept quiet, even wondered if it would prove effective? How many times, in her silence, had it been as if she participated in the rituals herself?

If only she wasn't so weak.

Avigail took a step away from Odelia. "You need not worry over me. Worry over yourself and how any man will want you if you keep up your prudish ways."

The words stung. But Odelia forced a small smile. "If the Lord does not intend for me to marry, I will accept that fate." She did not know of any worthy man to marry anyway. "Good night, Avigail."

Her cousin did not answer, and Odelia returned to her rooftop, the heady scent of incense still lingering in the air.

Odelia passed through the market, its stalls filled with useless wares. For who needed a wooden spoon without food to stir or a hyssop broom without crumbs to sweep?

She entered the Great Court of the Lord's house, passing the temple guards, seeking out the chest in which to drop her meager offering. The weaver had paid her for the work of three wicker baskets the day before, and since she'd finished her monthly course two days ago and purified herself in the *mikveh*, she'd been eager to make a trip to the temple.

She deposited her coins and sought a space off to the left where she could just glimpse the entrance to the Court of the Israelites and the stairs leading up to the Bronze Altar, the place where the high priest made sacrifices for the people. She tightened her prayer shawl about her shoulders, glancing beyond the Bronze Altar to the huge pillars on either side of the Holy Place. As a woman—even as the daughter of a temple priest—she would never get closer to the Holy of Holies than this. Never get closer to the *Shekinah*, the divine radiance of *El Shaddai's* spirit. Her abba told of the Holy Place decorated with beautiful etchings of flowers, trees, and fruits—priceless symbols of Eden. Of the thick blue curtain, embroidered in gold thread with cherubim representing the heavens and the Holy of Holies beyond. What would it be like to be in the presence of God?

She knelt, bowing her head to the smooth mosaic tile. She breathed deeply, attempting to push aside her empty belly and muscle aches to center her thoughts on Adonai. But even then, instead of prayer, Odelia's encounter with Avigail came to mind.

Her cousin believed she could enter the presence of the queen of heaven by burning incense, making cakes, and spilling blood. Would Odelia willingly spill her own blood if it meant being able to enter the Holy of Holies—or even the Holy Place, with its golden lampstand and table of showbread…? Anything that would put her just a bit closer to knowing Yahweh's presence?

She blinked, chastising herself. What was wrong with her that she became obsessed with such thoughts? Had not Adonai heard the cries of Hannah when she prayed in the temple at Shiloh? And yet a priest had interceded for her. A priest. One like her abba? If so, she would take her chances that Adonai's ears could discern her pleas through the sturdy walls of the Holy Place and past the thick curtain of the Holy of Holies.

And what would she ask of Him?

For a husband? Perhaps. More so, she'd ask for a friend. Someone who understood the struggles of her heart, someone who would not judge her for the weakness of her faith, someone who could see how badly she *wanted* to place her trust in Adonai but how she often struggled to do so.

Or better yet, she could pray for a strong faith—a faith as sturdy and bold as Jeremiah's.

Adonai, God of my salvation, even my prayers are aimless. Lead me.

After a long while, she lifted her head, meeting friendly gray eyes. A smile softened her lips, and her heart shifted into place.

Shaphan.

The older priest who served as a secretary in the temple was like a *saba* to her. When Odelia's abba would take her to the Lord's house as a girl, Shaphan would slip her honey cakes and raisin pastries. He engaged her with stories of Abraham and Moses and Joshua while her abba attended his duties inside the temple.

Shaphan had been old then. Now, he appeared ancient with his thick gray beard, his violet robe seeming to dwarf his shrunken frame. Best known for bringing the recovered scroll of the Law to Josiah, he had become a legend in her mind until she became comforted not by his notoriety but by his simple yet gracious spirit.

He shuffled closer, placed a hand on her head, and spoke a blessing over her. When he removed his hand, he lowered his voice. "Child, may we speak?"

She rose, her knees sore from kneeling on the polished marble. "Of course."

With his cane tapping gently on the marble floors of the Great Court, he led her past the Music Gate and the Chamber of Lepers to a room just off the upper courtyard, near the New Gate entrance. He opened the ornate oak door and entered.

Odelia hesitated, looking around, half expecting her abba to jump out from behind a column and demand to know what she was doing.

"Do not fear, child. This is the temple room of my son, Gemariah. Come."

She swallowed and slipped into a room with tall marble pillars, several clay lamps, a couch with fine cushions, and a wooden bench. She stopped short at the sight of the high priest in his elegant priestly garb. His ephod surpassed even the king's in beauty—gorgeously crafted colors of blue, scarlet, purple, and gold. The *miter* he wore upon his head with the gold plate, inscribed with the words *Holiness unto the Lord*, caused her throat to dry.

Three other priests, one captain of the guard with a leather breastplate and captain's robe, and a young man with probing eyes, his simple vestments and turban indicating him to be a priest in training, completed the circle. Odelia's skin prickled and she shifted where she stood, drawing her prayer shawl more tightly around her shoulders.

She glanced at Shaphan. What was the meaning of such an invitation? Were they not fearful she would defile them in this space?

Shaphan shut the door before turning to his guests. "You may sit."

The men did so, and Odelia looked around for a water basin to wash their feet. Nothing.

"Odelia, please sit." Shaphan gestured to a striped red-and-blue cushion.

She did not obey.

"Do not fear, child."

The repeated words did little to calm her. She lowered herself to the cushion. Shaphan remained standing. "We have invited you here, Odelia, to ask for your help."

Odelia swallowed. What need could they have of her—a small maiden who should have been married long ago?

Shaphan lowered himself to the wooden bench with rigid movements. "The Babylonians will attack soon, there is no mistaking that. We need to transport an item of value through the tunnels under the city before they break our walls. Several items, in fact."

So, Shaphan did not write off the danger of the Babylonians as her abba and Avigail did.

And yet, what did any of this have to do with her?

"I understand you are familiar with the tunnels and waterways beneath the city." Shaphan raised a bushy gray brow in her direction, his words a statement rather than a question. Odelia's face heated and sweat gathered beneath her tunic, the need for air consuming her constricted lungs.

How could he know such information? Odelia, Avigail, and Joash—Avigail's brother—had never told anyone about their adventures. "My lord?"

"Would you be willing to help us on this most important mission?"

They did not chastise her. They wanted her *help*.

She dared a glance at the young man close to her own age. He was strangely familiar, and though a warmth filled her belly at his intense stare, she couldn't place him. One corner of his mouth lifted almost imperceptibly, as if to encourage her.

She wet her lips. "My lord, I am your servant, of course, but I am not sure my abba—"

"Your abba must not know of what we discuss." This from the high priest, a tremble in his voice. "We need your word that what we speak of in this room will not leave it."

Odelia's gaze flew to Shaphan. She'd trust him with her life, but this secrecy? What had driven him to such desperate measures? What was he so anxious to save from the Babylonian army?

More importantly, how could she, an insignificant maiden whose abba would be furious should he learn of her involvement, be the one to lead such a holy group out of Jerusalem?

CHAPTER TWO

Odelia opened her mouth to speak, but to her horror, no words came forth.

The high priest straightened his regal form. "This is a fool's errand, Shaphan. And one I am beginning to think will not be blessed by the Lord." He speared Odelia with a penetrating gaze. "You are dismissed, Daughter."

She rose to leave but was stayed by Shaphan's gentle hand. "My lord, I beg of you to allow her to stay. She is a vital part of our plan."

The high priest stood. "A plan I am afraid I am no longer behind. I must pray about this longer. As I do, I am certain I will revert to my original statement of faith—Adonai will protect the temple and His people. He will honor us when we hold fast to His city and trust in His house. May He show mercy on me for doubting Him."

And then he was gone, the solid oak door closing behind him with an eerie echo that squeezed only a shekel of tension from the room.

"What now, Abba?" A priest her abba's age addressed Shaphan. This must be Gemariah then.

Shaphan tapped the olive staff he used for balance on the cedar wood floor. "The ark of the Lord was at Shiloh too. And it was not spared."

A chill chased up Odelia's spine at the mention of the ark. And of Shiloh. Only miles north in Israel, Shiloh was now a province of Assyria. Though once the home of both Samuel and Yahweh's tabernacle, the very one where Hannah prayed, it was now nothing but a pile of rocks and dirt. Hadn't Jeremiah prophesied that His house in Jerusalem would meet the same fate?

Shaphan tapped his cane on the floor again, twice, this time with more force. "The people have made the temple into an idol. The weak and vulnerable are oppressed. Injustice has become the law of the land. Why, even the slaves the king released were recaptured and put back in shackles. Adonai has become nothing more than a token of good fortune, and though it grieves my heart to say it, Jeremiah is right. We can no longer pretend the Babylonians will turn back. They are at our walls. The Middle Gate already weakens. We are thirsty and hungry. If we wish to spare the ark of the covenant, we do not have much time."

"How will we transport it? Especially now, without the high priest?" This time, the soldier spoke. The royal colors he wore told of the kingly courts, the lion of the tribe of Judah embroidered on his cloak. But Odelia could not ponder how he came to be in such company with his words still lingering in the stiff room.

They meant to move the ark. By means of the tunnels.

The ark of the covenant. The ark, which was not to be touched by anyone except for the ceremonially clean high priest, and only once a year at that.

Odelia's hands shook, emboldening her to speak. "What of Uzzah?" she whispered.

Uzzah, the man who had put out his hand to steady the ark when the oxen stumbled during the transporting of it by David to Jerusalem. Yahweh had struck him dead.

The young priest with the piercing eyes spoke this time. "The ark was treated irreverently, the Law disregarded. This time, Levitical priests will carry the covered ark with poles upon their own shoulders."

"Through the narrow confines and sludge of the underground tunnels?" The callousness of what they planned to do loosened her tongue. Surely they would all be struck dead for their irreverence. "Forgive me. But I have been in the tunnels. They are not always pleasant. I have seen rats more than once. And the tunnels grow narrow in spots, too narrow to allow for the ark." Never mind poles and priests.

Shaphan cleared his throat. "Now might be a time for introductions. This is Odelia, daughter of Pashhur. Odelia, meet Aden, son of Baruch, secretary to Jeremiah." He introduced the rest of the people in the room, but she could not get past the introduction of the young man with the soulful eyes. This man knew the prophet himself. His abba, Baruch, was a close friend and scribe to Jeremiah—had even boldly read Jeremiah's prophecies in the temple years ago, which led to King Jehoiakim reading them aloud and burning the scrolls Baruch had labored on for years, slice by slice. And yet, Baruch was not a Levite—how then could his son be training as a priest?

Either way, she should not have spoken so brazenly. Aden likely held her in little regard, seeing as her own abba had harshly punished Jeremiah all those years ago.

Gemariah turned to Aden. "Have you spoken to Baruch or Jeremiah about this? His prophecies command that we surrender to the Babylonians. Will Adonai bless our endeavor to save the ark of His presence and the temple treasures not taken in the invasion ten years ago?"

Gemariah's humility in addressing the younger man caused Aden to grow in her own estimation. She loved Shaphan and his family. If his son, a priest, respected Aden as a messenger of Jeremiah, perhaps Odelia should too.

"Jeremiah is imprisoned in the courtyard of the guard in the royal palace by the king." Aden's gaze traveled to the soldier, and a smile flickered across his face. "Uncle Seraiah here tries to watch out for him, but Jeremiah's conditions are not pleasant. Not that any of ours will be soon." For the first time, Odelia noticed a clay jar Aden held in his hands. "My abba oversaw a land purchase Jeremiah made from his cousin, a field in Anathoth. Seventeen whole shekels. The entire courtyard ridiculed him and my abba."

Aden lifted the jar. "The deed is here. Jeremiah ordered my abba to seal it away and preserve it as a symbol that one day, our people will again own property on this land, will buy and sell houses and vineyards and fields. It is a promise of our future hope. When my abba asked Jeremiah about the ark, he was insistent that it would not be a vital part of Adonai's future covenant, and yet he did see honor in preserving it from the impending army. Unlike Hananiah, he is certain that nothing in the city will be left for us to return to."

Odelia's mind spun even as a deep sadness filled her being. A future without the ark? Without the temple? Where then would her people worship? Perhaps her abba was right in thinking Jeremiah a false prophet.

She thought of the high priest's certainty that Yahweh would defend His people if they stayed put and clung to the temple. And yet, he did not seem overly concerned about Shaphan's group going through with their plan to remove the ark. Wouldn't the high priest care about such things?

"I believe it the right course of action, as we have already discussed at length. Does anyone have reservations?" Shaphan looked around the group, but none spoke. "Daughter, will you help us?"

Odelia glanced at her hands, folded in her lap. "I have only made it to the end of the tunnels once. Our lamps burned out, or we feared our immas would miss us. There are many outlets and I—I am not confident I would not lead you directly to the Babylonians at our gates."

The tunnels below Jerusalem were said to be used by King David when he captured the city from the Canaanites. The king's men had gone up through the outlets and into the city, surprising the unsuspecting Canaanites.

The royal soldier named Seraiah cleared his throat. "The men I would send are not strangers to scouting out land. I am confident that with your guidance and their skill, we would be able to stay clear of the invading army."

"Our aim is to travel under the Babylonians and into the Valley of Jehoshaphat, where we believe King David entered the tunnels in his attack. From there, it is our hope to follow the river east, away from the City of David." Shaphan's words caused a chill to travel up Odelia's spine.

East. A direction symbolic of exile and banishment. East, away from the City of David. If she didn't respect Shaphan and his judgment so very much...

And yet... "What of the tunnels themselves? They are incredibly narrow in spots. I could pass through them when I was younger and smaller, but how is the ark of His presence to fit through?"

Not that she had ever seen the ark herself, but she had heard its description read to the people from the scroll of Exodus. One and a half cubits in breadth. Much larger than her own breadth even now.

Seraiah cast her an appraising look before directing his words to Shaphan. "I can see why you think much of this one, Shaphan. She has the courage to speak her mind."

Odelia tried not to blush beneath his praise as the imposing soldier turned to her. "My men will go prepared with tools to widen the tunnel if necessary. Our bigger concern is that any sound they make in doing so will not travel up to our enemy. They will have to muffle it as best as they are able."

It seemed this man and Shaphan held all the answers to her questions. And yet, why then the hitch in her spirit? "How soon will you go?"

"Soon," Shaphan said. "The moon grows bright. A darkening moon is an ill time to begin a journey."

"And when can I expect to return?"

Shaphan exchanged a glance with the soldier Seraiah. "You should not plan to return."

Her hands trembled in her lap.

Could she do what they asked of her? Lead a group of such elite men out of the city through the Canaanite tunnels? And what of her family, her home? What would happen to everything she knew and loved if she left it all to the invading army?

"We will meet again tomorrow at this time to discuss more details." Shaphan addressed the room. "Thank you all for coming."

Odelia rose as the men left, each of them giving her a small bow or smile before leaving the room. When Aden passed with his earthenware jar in hand, he dipped his head, and she noticed the slight depression in one cheek that seemed to ally itself with the sparkle in his eyes.

When she moved to follow them, Shaphan stayed her with a hand before closing the door. "May I speak to you plainly, Daughter?"

"Of course."

"I love you like a granddaughter, and so it is with some selfishness that I hope you will agree to this task. It grieves my heart to think of you here when the Babylonians knock down our walls. They will not be kind. And although Jeremiah foretells of the blessing that will come to those exiles who will be deported, it will not be for many years."

"Shaphan, I want to accompany you, but—"

"Child, I will not be taking the trip."

Her jaw fell. "What?"

"I am ancient, Daughter. The tunnels are no place for an old man. I will only slow the progress. In fact, none in the room today will be going, save for Aden. Their presence is too prominent, their absence too easily noticed. We are praying for God to use each one in Babylon if they survive the siege."

"And what of you?" A walnut-sized lump formed in her throat at the thought of never seeing Shaphan again. He would be unable to make the long trek north to Babylon.

"Yahweh has told me my days on earth will end before the Babylonians break through the Middle Gate."

"Oh, Shaphan!" She did not think about what laws she broke as she hurled herself into his frail arms.

He squeezed her tight, and in his embrace she felt all the fatherly love she had never known from her own abba. "Yahweh is a God of hope, Daughter. I am trusting His plans for our people and for each of us. Stay faithful to Him."

She released the precious man, fighting the urge to wipe her nose with the sleeve of her prayer shawl. An intense sorrow threatened to overtake her. It sat in the shadows of the room as if stalking its prey. "What will happen to Abba and Imma, to the rest of my family?"

"The entire fate of Judah would be better if we surrendered, even now, to the Babylonians."

"Could they—I mean, could we invite them to come beneath the tunnels?"

"Daughter, you know that is not possible. Your abba would tell the king as soon as he heard of such plans, and the ark and what remains of the temple treasures would be left for loot."

She hung her head. She knew this, of course, but how could she leave her family without at least trying to spare them?

"I will go." She supposed she knew all along that this would be her answer, but once she voiced the words, the shadows receded from the frayed edges of her spirit. In the end, how could she neglect a calling from Adonai?

Shaphan smiled a wobbly, ancient smile that showed a missing tooth. "Thank you, child. The journey will not be easy, but I trust the Lord will honor it."

"When should I prepare to depart?"

"Two days."

She swallowed. "So soon?"

"We are unsure where the tunnels will land you, therefore we do not know how long it will take you to reach your destination or what obstacles you will encounter. The moon will be at its fullest by the time you make your way out of the tunnels. At least, that is our hope."

"Should I return tomorrow?"

"Yes. There is much to discuss about provisions. But Odelia, I must reiterate that it is imperative no one knows about this undertaking."

She heard so plainly what he was saying. She could not allow her parents to suspect anything, even as she prepared to leave the only home she had ever known.

"I understand."

He took her face in his hands. "Now, Daughter, may Adonai bless you and keep you. May He make His face shine upon you and be gracious to you. May He turn His face toward you and give you peace."

A sob worked its way loose from her chest and up into her throat, where it erupted in the holy room. "I will miss you so very much," she whispered.

He kissed her forehead. "Yahweh will replant what He tears down. It is there, in His kingdom, that we put our trust. Go in peace, Daughter."

She fled from the room without looking back, exiting the temple while hiding her tear-soaked face in her shawl, Shaphan's words tucked in the corners of her mind.

"Go in peace, Daughter."

She would do this. She would leave everything she'd ever known and give herself over to the bowels of the earth beneath her beloved city, allowing those dark, cold tunnels to spill her out into an unknown land, an unknown future.

She would do it for the sake of her people and her heritage, for the sake of the precious symbol of her faith. And yet the question remained—how to claim peace while doing all of this?

CHAPTER THREE

Odelia kept her head down as she scurried through the paved streets of the northern part of the city, the dust from the thirsty roads swirling into her face as a merchant in an oxcart passed.

She coughed and turned down her street but not before glimpsing the archway into the lower city, where news of more and more deaths due to the siege reached her ears daily.

Not for the first time, Odelia considered how her abba's priestly station ensured that they lived in the more prosperous part of town. And although she'd never knowingly aided in the great divide between rich and poor in the city, it seemed to matter little now that starvation threatened them all. They were bound together in hunger.

When she saw the tiny urchin—a beggar who looked to be no more than a pile of skin and bones—leaning against the column several steps from the entrance to her family's courtyard, her heart leaped.

"Hashem." She knelt beside the dirty nine-year-old. "Have you been waiting long?"

He shook his head, a smile inching up his dry face. "I wait all day for you if it means a scrap of bread."

She dug in the pocket of her tunic for the generous piece of barley bread she had stored there from her own plate that morning. Although *generous* was perhaps a bit too substantial a word for the lump in her hands. Her own stomach rumbled at the feel of the wholesome grain. She unwrapped the flax cloth and offered it to the boy.

He took it, closing his eyes in what looked to be a prayer of thanksgiving before tearing off a piece and shoving it in his mouth. How she wished she had some of the honey cakes she used to give him before the siege began. He had loved those. The first time she gifted him one, he'd shoved the entire morsel in his mouth. As the days and months wore on, however, he learned to savor the bits she took from her own plate.

"Thank you." His teeth showed, contrasting with his dark skin.

The boy had been brought to the city by an Ammonite horse breeder. When river fever from their travels struck Hashem and he could not carry the water buckets, the Ammonite left him in the city to die.

Odelia had found him in the dirt near the city wall, shaking and trembling with fever. She borrowed the cart of a sympathetic pottery maker to transport Hashem to her abba's home.

Though Imma had not allowed the dirty outsider child past their threshold, she had allowed him to stay in their courtyard. Odelia set him on her own bedroll beneath the palm tree then brought blankets to him and ladled bone broth into his mouth.

When Abba came home from the temple that day, he'd been livid, demanding the unclean Ammonite be sent back from where he came.

"But Abba, he is sick and has no one to care for him. Please allow him to stay." She'd bowed low to her abba, careful to keep her body well beneath his fine linen girdle in order to show her reverence, beseeching him with every humbled muscle in her body.

"Daughter, I am a temple priest. I cannot be defiled by an uncircumcised Gentile whose ancestors are enemies of our people."

She kept her head low, knowing her next words risked her abba's wrath. "Forgive me for persisting, Abba, but what of the Lord's command to Moses to love the foreigner as ourselves and treat them as our native-born?"

The blow was swift, the toe of Abba's sandal landing directly in her rib, the *tzitzit* of his prayer shawl fluttering to settle alongside his cloak. "Get up." Her abba's words were deep and menacing and she used a nearby bench to pull herself to standing, the bones in her middle aching.

"Do not quote Scripture to *me*, Daughter. You do not even know how to read—you remember the words incorrectly. Perhaps instead you should pray on Yahweh's fifth commandment."

"Yes, Abba," she squeaked out, barely able to meet his gaze but seeing the faint drops of sweat upon his brow where he had tied his phylactery—a small leather box that held Scripture, a very literal way to obey Moses's command to bind the Law on their foreheads.

"See the boy out and make sure to wash your bedding thoroughly before bringing it back into our home."

With much struggle, she managed to transition the boy back into the oxcart. She carried him to the only place she could think of—Shaphan's home.

The old priest did not hesitate to take Hashem in, and he and his wife cared for the boy until the child recovered. These days, Hashem still found a ready place at Shaphan's table. After the boy recovered from his fever, Odelia visited the older priest often. One day, she asked him to quote the passage in Leviticus about loving the foreigner. He did.

Abba was wrong. Odelia had remembered the words perfectly. Worse, she had a suspicion he knew it. But why would her abba twist the holy words to suit his own preferences?

That was the beginning of a curtain being lifted from her eyes. She noted her abba's holy habits were often devoid of a deeper commitment—devoid of love. She noted her imma's worship of Ba'al and the queen of heaven, how Abba knew of such things but did not rebuke her.

She blinked, focusing on the young Ammonite boy in front of her. Now, thank Adonai, Hashem was as healthy as could be amid a drought and famine.

He chewed the bread she'd given him carefully. "Have I ever told you you are my favorite woman?"

She laughed, still surprised at the turn of phrases that came from the boy's mouth. "And you are my favorite boy." They began walking up the street, side by side. She bit the inside of her cheek after a few moments and stopped to kneel beside him, staring into his dark eyes. "Hashem..." But what to say? Shaphan had commanded her not to tell anyone she was leaving. And yet what of the boy's fate?

"I spoke to Shaphan today. He is not feeling well. I think a visit from you would be good."

Would Adonai punish her for her lie? Yet, if Shaphan could direct the boy on how best to escape perishing at the hands of the Babylonians, he would.

"I will go there now. Last time, his cook gave me some mulled wine." He licked his lips.

"Tell him I sent you."

"I will. Do you need any messages delivered today?" Hashem often thanked her for her small offerings by running messages or conducting minor chores for her. Once, before the siege, he'd picked an entire basket of reeds for her. She'd soaked them and made several baskets, fetching a fair price with the merchant who sold them at market.

"Not today."

"I will take my leave then."

Without thinking, she grasped the boy in her arms. He wiggled beneath her grip, pulled out of her embrace, and straightened his dirtied tunic, looking anxiously up the street to see if anyone had seen her display of affection. "I have a reputation to keep, woman."

She giggled, but her joy was immediately squelched by the reminder of how much she would miss his proud, at times surprisingly humble, demeanor. Would he worry over her? And when the Babylonians invaded... How might they treat a foreign orphan?

She tried to picture Hashem in Babylon with her friends who had been taken during the deportation. Should she give him their names?

"Listen, Hashem." Her serious tone caused inquisitive eyes to study her. "If you cannot find me soon, do not worry. When the Babylonians break our walls, willingly surrender to them. They will take kindlier to you."

"Odelia?"

But she turned her face away so he could not see her tears, her weakness. "Go to Shaphan, now."

She had to trust that the old priest would know how much to tell the boy.

Without warning, Hashem threw his arms around her waist and clutched tight. She pressed his little body close to hers. "Go, now," she whispered. "Shalom, shalom, Hashem."

Perfect peace.

He raced away, and she slipped into her family's courtyard. Her imma's rose of Sharon, normally green and vibrant and ready to flower this time of year, raised brown, withered branches to the sky, as if beseeching the heavens for a drop of rain.

After putting her fingers to her lips and touching the mezuzah fixed upon the doorpost, Odelia entered her home. Imma pulled a meager loaf of barley bread from the oven and set it down on the oak table.

"It is the last of it," she said by way of greeting. "Perhaps you will go to the market tomorrow and see what you can find."

Odelia nodded as she used the precious little water by the threshold to wipe the dust from her feet. "Of course." She moved to the bowl at the table and dipped her hands, drying them on a clean rag.

"You were at the temple a long time today. I needed your help with the laundering."

Was there water left for such things? "I am sorry, Imma. I will help you tomorrow."

Tomorrow, her last day at home.

"What does one small wisp of a girl have so much to pray about?"

Odelia studied her imma, her head covering tied in a severe knot at the base of her neck, reminding Odelia of the hard, strict edges of the woman. She did not wish to lie, especially to her imma, but Shaphan's words seemed to cloak every precious syllable from her mouth. She *was* praying for a long time before he called her into the inner rooms. She would focus on that.

"I pray for many things, especially when I have been away so long after my moon time."

"Avigail visited today. She swears by offering libations to the queen of heaven. Said her imma was blessed by extra flour in the barrel this morning after offering such to her yesterday."

"Imma, you cannot possibly think—"

Imma let a hand fall to the table. "My family grows hungry. My head aches more than before. Our throats are dry and our lips parched. Can you blame me, Daughter, for looking elsewhere to provide for us?"

"Adonai will deliver us if we listen to Him. If we would surrender to—" She stopped at seeing her imma's wide eyes aimed at the doorpost.

She turned to see Abba, who stepped inside and stopped near the bowl. He lifted his priestly robes, and Odelia rushed to wash his feet.

"Shalom, family."

"Shalom, Abba."

"Shalom, Husband." Imma set a small cube of soft cheese on a clay plate in the center of the table. "It is all we have."

"Ilana, please do not complain the moment I touch the mezuzah. And what is this talk about surrendering to the Babylonians, Daughter?"

Odelia scurried to fetch the earthenware cups from the cupboard. She poured the last of their beer into the three cups. As she did so, Aden's earthenware jar came to mind.

Aden's words at the meeting with Shaphan and the other men came back to her. *"It is a promise of our future hope."* How could a paltry piece of land in Anathoth, purchased for a mere seventeen shekels, symbolize such a grand promise?

Even she knew that many in the city were in favor of surrendering to the Babylonians. But the king was not. And although a mess of political factions had taken over Jerusalem, in the end, there was no political stance that mattered, save the king's.

She gathered a breath. "I heard talk at the temple today that the prophet Jeremiah believes the worst of Jerusalem's fate will be spared even now if we surrender to the Babylonians. He urges us to yield, to enter the foreign country and seek its welfare. Pray for it, even."

Imma released a sarcastic huff. "Pray for our enemies? Ridiculous."

Abba cast a stern look her way. "I refuse to allow such talk of disloyalty to Adonai beneath the roof of my house. Do you understand, Odelia?"

Her shoulders drooped. "Yes, Abba."

"We must put our faith in the temple. The Israelites did not have Yahweh's dwelling when the Assyrians came—we do. Adonai will not allow such destruction of His dwelling."

For a moment, listening to her abba's certain words, she doubted Shaphan and Jeremiah and Aden. After all, the high priest himself thought as her abba did. Ten years ago, when the Babylonians came upon their city, they had spared the temple, taking only some of its treasures along with the best artisans, soldiers, and scholars in the city. How could two groups be so certain of entirely opposing beliefs?

"I would put your thoughts on other matters. I have spoken to the woodworker, Adino, today. We came to an agreement concerning your future."

Imma straightened. "You have agreed on a *mohar*?"

Odelia's legs trembled. "You wish me to marry Adino?" The woodworker stank of uncleanliness, and the last time Imma had sent her to pay him for a table, he had brushed up so close to Odelia that she found her back to the wall, his rotten breath on her face.

"You could do worse, Daughter."

"I could do better in not marrying at all! Adino is older than you, Abba. I have grown up with his children, and what is more, he favors his beer far more than his prayer shawl."

The sting that ran a line of fire across her cheek shocked her. She raised a hand to her face. Abba had not struck her since the day she'd brought Hashem home. He had not slapped her face since before her time of womanhood.

"Your tongue is too loose. It is not fitting for a daughter of Adonai."

She bowed her head, shame replacing the gnawing hunger in her stomach that the square of soft cheese and crust of barley bread could not fill. "Forgive me, Abba."

"You will find favor with Adino, Daughter." Imma placed her hand on her daughter's arm. "You will bear children, and they will be your comfort."

Odelia bit her tongue, something Abba commanded during childhood when she was tempted to allow her every thought to slip past loose lips. How could they wish to send her away to that man?

Then she remembered. In two more sunsets, she planned to leave Abba and Imma forever. To participate in an unthinkable task, one she prayed Adonai would bless. In the time of two sunsets, it would not matter if Abba had drawn up a betrothal contract to Adino if the bride no longer lived beneath her abba's roof.

The rest of their evening meal was quiet, and after she helped Imma clean and listened to Abba read the Torah, she slipped into her bedchamber, grateful to be alone with her thoughts.

As she lay on her pallet, she curled her body facing the temple. She prayed for Adonai's guidance. And although she didn't hear an audible answer, she did feel a drawing of her spirit. Not to Abba and his unyielding, determined ways and strict rules but to Shaphan's loving-kindness, to the prayer he'd spoken over her as a blessing, to the light in Aden's eyes as he spoke of the future promise of hope held in a simple earthenware vessel.

And she knew. She knew she would follow through with her plans to help Shaphan's group lead the ark of the covenant through the tunnels beneath the city.

"Adonai, know my heart," she whispered into her blankets as the star-studded sky cast down faint light upon her from the high window of her bedchamber. For in the end, she was not sure of this plan, or even of her weak faith. But in the end, she trusted Yahweh, the God of the earth, with her heart.

CHAPTER FOUR

Two nights later, Odelia slid from her bedchamber onto the dusty streets, carrying nothing but a satchel holding a small flask of water, an extra tunic, a small blanket, a lamp with an extra flask of oil, two figs, and a crust of bread.

Doubts assailed her as she kept to the shadows of the homes along her street.

She felt like a thief, stealing away from her parents in the dead of night. An ungrateful, disobedient thief. For though her parents had never been overly affectionate and at times were downright cruel, they were still her abba and imma. They had provided for her all these years. Imma had taught her the art of basket weaving. Abba had recited Scripture to her so she could be familiar with the Lord's laws. Sometimes, he would even smile at her as if he were almost pleased.

And now, she would never see them again. What would happen to them once the Babylonians broke through the city wall? Would they be hurt? Killed? Or would they be taken as exiles to Babylon like so many of their friends ten years before? Would they make a new life without her?

Halfway to the temple, she almost turned to retrace her steps and creep back into her bedchamber. She imagined snuggling into her familiar bedroll but could not glean any comfort from the image.

For when she woke to the light of the sun the next morning, she'd regret not following through with this most important duty. She'd regret not keeping her word to Shaphan.

The moon glowed in the shape of an archer's bow, shedding enough light for Odelia to creep through the streets. The faint scent of incense on rooftops met her nostrils, adding to her nauseousness. Yesterday, during their secret meeting, they had agreed to meet at the Siloam Pool, where the entrance to the Canaanite Tunnel could be found. The priests and the men Seraiah had enlisted to help, along with Shaphan and Aden, would bring the temple treasures.

That is, if all went according to their plan.

When Odelia saw the small, quiet crowd at the edge of the wide steps to the pool, she breathed a sigh of relief and almost wept at the sight of women and several small children.

The priests were bringing their families. Though Odelia hadn't been certain, she wondered how the men would manage leaving behind their wives and children to the fate of the Babylonians. She started down the steps, searching out Shaphan, when a small finger poked her side.

A sound of pure joy bubbled up in her throat. "Hashem!" She threw her arms around the grinning boy.

"I am not sure if I should be happy to see you or mad that you planned to leave me alone in this city." His eyes twinkled in the light of the moon reflecting from the pool.

"I would have rather drunk a gallon of fish oil than to leave you in such a way, but I gave Shaphan my word. I am so glad he invited you along." She kept her voice low, cognizant that attracting attention at the start would do no good.

"A secret mission beneath the city tunnels to outsmart the Babylonians and save Adonai's ark? I cannot think of anything better!"

Odelia smiled at the boy's enthusiasm. He'd adopted the ways of her people a year ago, even asking Shaphan to circumcise him—not an easy ask for anyone, certainly not for a young boy. "I have no doubt you will be a true asset to our undertaking."

She looked at the crowd and noticed many lowering themselves to their knees in a posture of reverence. Her mouth fell open. A thin sheen of sweat broke out over her skin at the sight of four priests carrying a large object on poles atop their shoulders. She took in the unmistakable bulge of the most holy treasure beneath a cloth of blue, the shielding curtain and durable leather the priests covered it with unable to hide the outline of the wings of the two massive cherubim spreading over the ark.

She squinted, searching for some sign—a movement or shimmer of wind atop the ark—to indicate Adonai's presence. Nothing. And still, it did not cease to amaze her, for whether or not she could see Him, surely He *was* here. She willed her legs to move to join the others, but all she could do was drink in that solid blue cloth, awed by what lay beneath. The ark of the covenant. Jeremiah proclaimed there would come a time when Yahweh's presence would not be confined to the ark, when the box of acacia wood covered in gold would not be needed by the people to worship.

Had that time already come? Or was the very holiness of Adonai's mighty presence contained upon the mercy seat even now, settled upon the two cherubim that hid the commandments He'd given Moses, Aaron's budded staff, and a jar of manna from the wilderness?

Reminders of Yahweh's holiness, of the line of priesthood He'd bestowed upon her people, and of His ultimate provision. He had not struck the priests down for removing the ark, despite the absence of the high priest. No doubt, Shaphan chose them carefully. No doubt, they were each a believer of Jeremiah's prophecies.

Odelia didn't blink as she stared at the covered ark for several moments. Then an insatiable urge to join the others and bow before it overwhelmed her. She took Hashem's hand and pulled him down the stairs with the others, where they dropped to their knees.

They listened to Shaphan's quiet voice above them, beseeching Adonai for the success of their task, for their protection, for the courage they would each need in the days and months ahead. He begged Him to remember the sacrifices he'd offered the day before to cover the sins of the sojourners. He kept the prayer short, no doubt understanding the sight they might make if seen by the open pool.

After Shaphan finished, he spoke her name. Odelia jumped to attention, her skin heating beneath the crowd's gaze. She squeezed Hashem's hand and scurried forward to where the old man stood before the other priests, fully clothed in their fine priestly garments—shining white linen pants and tunic, their turbans one single long strip of fabric wound around their heads, and their long belts of blue, purple, scarlet, and pure white. She shuddered to think of their tunics brushing the sides of the ancient tunnels, of the clean white growing dirty. Would they be deemed unclean by Yahweh?

She had so many questions, and yet the crowd of thirty or so parted for her, spilling her out in front of Shaphan. Odelia bowed at his feet, her body trembling at her proximity to the ark of the covenant. She dared not look at it this closely, dared not possess such intimate audacity. For the ark had only known the inside of the Holy of Holies for the last several centuries. One danger of this task would be becoming too familiar with it, as Uzzah had done.

Shaphan cupped her face with ancient, gnarled hands. "Thank you for sending Hashem to me."

A bubble of emotion lodged in her throat. "Thank you for allowing him to come with us."

"We have already said our goodbyes, yes? You will take the lead with Aden. Seraiah's men will follow and then the priests holding the mercy seat." After more conversation, she understood that eight priests in total, not including Aden, would accompany them, likely all Shaphan could induce—or trust—to take up such a mission. Hopefully, the extra priests would be able to give the others a reprieve when they grew weary, or Adonai forbid, ill on their journey. She noted two priests holding the leather-covered table of showbread on poles and another the covered golden lampstand sitting upon a carrying frame.

She knew from their meeting a few days earlier that others in their company would be commissioned to carry the temple treasures not taken by the Babylonians during the deportation—the talents of pearls and gold tablets they could manage, as well as King David's lyres and lutes, all coated in gold. The two trumpets of hammered silver. Money from the temple treasury. It would help them along the river and, if Adonai saw to it that they made it that far, to a designated spot where they hoped to purchase necessary animals and supplies.

After the priests came more soldiers with supplies—tents and food and goat hair blankets and cooking pots and flasks of beer—then lastly, the women and children. It was a diverse group, one that was sure to draw attention if they chose a wrong tunnel and did not land far enough away from the Babylonian army. And they all depended on her to guide them.

After Shaphan gave her one final embrace and Aden did the same with his uncle Seraiah, Odelia breathed in the last of the open air inside the City of David. "Adonai, direct my senses." She entered the tunnel with her small lamp, Aden close behind.

She wondered if the Babylonians had discovered this tunnel when they broke into the city ten years ago. If so, had they explored it and blocked the exits? Would their group reach the end only to find the tunnel obstructed by immovable rock? Or worse, by fierce Babylonian guards?

She shivered, attempting to cast her fear aside. The Babylonians had been more interested in searching out the educated and elite in Jerusalem and taking them into exile. They'd been more interested in ransacking what they could of the temple treasures. Surely they hadn't taken the time to explore every nook and cranny of their city, especially one rumored to have been blocked by royal officials.

Odelia and Aden walked in silence for several moments, the bedrock around them wide at the beginning of the tunnel. He smelled of cypress and hyssop, a comforting scent that served to calm her quivering stomach.

Her lamp bounced shadows off the walls. The scent of cool, damp earth surrounded them. She tried not to dwell on her parents, sleeping in the home she grew up in. Abba would be furious when he discovered her missing. As a priest, would he also realize other priests were missing? Would he understand what happened? Would he question Shaphan?

A band of sadness wrapped around her chest at the thought of the man who had been closer than a grandfather to her. Her lungs tightened with emotion, and she pressed it back and down, desperate to overcome it. The tunnels, with their little oxygen, were not a place to succumb to anxiety. She was the leader of this group, a protector of the ark. She must be brave.

"How often have you been in these tunnels, did you say?" Aden spoke from behind.

"Often. My cousins and I would sneak away. I do not know how Shaphan knew of our escapades."

She heard the smile in Aden's words. "That man is a prophet himself, I should say. When I was little, I heard that my abba was reading Jeremiah's scrolls in the temple. I was fearful he would be punished, and I intended to interrupt him, but Shaphan met me at the temple gate. Somehow, he talked me out of my plans. I never could understand why he was waiting for me outside the entrance instead of listening to my abba read the scrolls."

"What did he say to dissuade you?"

"He told me that Yahweh's plans are often not in line with our own. That they were sometimes difficult to bear but always intended for the ultimate good of His glory."

Odelia winced. "A tough lesson for one so young."

"But one I needed to hear."

She kept moving her feet, drawing the group deeper into the tunnel. "I am sorry your abba was not able to join us."

"He was able, but he will not leave Jeremiah in prison. He is a faithful friend." Did she detect something of bitterness in his tone, or was it her imagination?

"My abba is Pashhur, the one who had Jeremiah flogged and put in prison those many years ago." Best to get it out in the open now. She didn't want to hide shameful secrets with this man she may depend on for her life in the days to come.

"I know this."

"Oh." She stopped. Of course he did. Shaphan had introduced her as Pashhur's daughter on the first day of their meeting. "Are we moving too quickly for the others?"

He turned. "The soldiers are right behind us. I see their lamp."

She continued. "I would not blame you for doubting me, given my bloodline."

He didn't answer right away. Finally, he sighed. "I trust Shaphan. That is enough. Also, I have seen you in the temple often. I asked Shaphan about you long ago."

The blood rushed to her face. At least he would not see her blush in the dark of the tunnels. "You—you did?"

"I have not seen one so doggedly faithful in her prayers. I was curious." He spoke the words simply, as if his interest was nothing to be embarrassed over.

"I—I do not remember seeing you." She could have slapped herself for the lame, but honest, response.

"I do not suspect you would, seeing your face was always pressed to the floor."

She laughed. "I go to the temple to pray, not to ogle those who have come to worship." Immediately, she regretted the words. "Forgive me. Abba says I have a weak tongue. It is why I do not yet have a husband."

Again, her words went before her.

"Not to disrespect your abba, but I find it refreshing. Better not to guess what is on your mind. We have many hours ahead of us, I should think."

They grew quiet before she spoke again. "Do you think we will ever pray in the temple again?"

Did he hear her unspoken words? Would they ever see Jerusalem again? Would they ever know the familiarity of their homes, their families?

"Jeremiah foretells that our people will not be brought back for seventy years from when the first captives were taken. That puts me at the age of eighty-two. Perhaps I will be blessed to live so long."

"Sixty more years," she whispered. If he was correct, then her parents, if they survived the siege, would not live to see such a homecoming. She may not live to see it. And even if she did, would the temple still stand?

"It becomes narrow up ahead." She raised her lamp to where the tunnel grew incredibly slim. She picked her footing carefully, as the caves were uneven in places, making one liable to trip. Aden would see her on her face for an altogether different reason than he had in the temple.

He turned, speaking to the soldier directly behind him, who did not waste time positioning their hammers and axes against the sides of the walls. Odelia and Aden slid past the narrow spot, waiting for the soldiers to work. The men wrapped linen rags around their tools when striking the bedrock to muffle the sound that might carry through the tunnel to Babylonian ears.

"Do you think we are outside the city yet?" Aden asked. They leaned against the walls, a few paces from where the soldiers worked.

It was the first time she glimpsed his handsome features lit by the flames of her lamp. Beneath the light, the tension on his face lay plain. Those piercing eyes drooped with a burden she very much wished to help him carry.

She shook her head. "No. When we travel beneath the Gihon Spring, we will likely see water. Then we will be outside the city walls and beneath the Kidron Valley. Hezekiah's tunnel runs parallel to this one, only it is much wetter." King Hezekiah had built the tunnel over a century earlier to help the city survive the Assyrian siege. He had blocked the upper spring of Gihon, bringing the water down through the tunnel, leaving the Canaanite tunnel they now traveled a much drier route than Hezekiah's.

"You certainly know your history."

"I find it fascinating, and when Abba reads the Scriptures, I try to piece it all together in my head. When he read of Hezekiah's work in the scroll of Chronicles and I told my cousins, they convinced me to come explore with them."

"I suppose you never thought you would be leading an expedition such as this."

She shook her head, the solid banging of the soldiers' tools jarring the little peace she clung to. "I did not. Forgive me, but may I ask... I am confused about your station. Are you a scribe or a priest?"

The corner of his mouth lifted. "I see I was correct in saying I would enjoy knowing what is on your mind rather than guessing at it."

She lifted a hand to her burning cheek.

"It is not an unreasonable question, considering my introduction as the son of Baruch."

Beside them, the soldiers chipped away at the tunnel walls.

"I was not born into the family of Baruch. My true name is Aden ben Lewek. My abba was a priest. He died eight months before my imma also died, giving birth to me."

Odelia let out a sympathetic groan. "How horrible. I am so sorry."

Aden sighed. "The remnant of my family was north in Israel when the Assyrians took it over. I was an orphan."

"What happened?"

"Shaphan took me in for a time, tried to find a priestly family in which I could make my home."

Odelia's heart twisted at his words, at the remembrance of kind Shaphan. It seemed Hashem was not the only orphan the older priest had cared for.

"I stayed with Shaphan and his wife for three days before the midwife who delivered me brought news of a babe's death. The babe of Jeremiah's scribe."

"Baruch."

Aden nodded. "Baruch's wife—the woman I think of as my imma—was happy to take me in and call me her own. My abba was less enthusiastic at first. But he now freely admits I have grown on him."

"I am so glad for you. It is an unusual arrangement though, is it not? You are the firstborn and destined for priesthood though the man who raised you is a scribe?"

"It is." Aden tapped a finger on the wall. "If you are being honest, then I would also like to be."

"Please."

"I find I am more gifted in the work of a scribe. But I am honored to do the work Adonai has bequeathed to me in my lineage."

She dug behind the meaning in his words, felt he tried to tell her he was more comfortable with parchment and ink than knife and lamb. "It is a great responsibility."

He gazed at her. "It is."

Odelia bit her lip. "Your imma… Baruch's wife. Is she among us?"

The cave grew tight with the silence between them before Aden finally answered. "She died some time ago."

He was leaving behind all his family as well. "I am sorry."

"Thank you."

And then, because for once her tongue was at a loss, she said, "Perhaps…perhaps we should pray while they work?"

One corner of Aden's mouth lifted. "You are unlike any woman I know, Odelia, daughter of Pashhur."

She bristled at her abba's name, despising that she should feel so many complicated feelings about her abba, that she should detest being identified with the man who flogged a prophet of God and was known for his harsh stinginess in his care of temple worshipers. At the same time, she ached that she would never see that man again.

She cleared her throat. "Shall we?"

He nodded, bowing his head. She sank into his whispered prayers for the city and people left behind, for the temple, for their group, and finally, for the safe delivering of the ark to its new destination.

But where was its new home? And how would her people worship in the presence of the ark if they were taken away to Babylon?

CHAPTER FIVE

After an interminable time, the soldiers broke the tunnel walls. They only traveled a few more feet, however, before having to stop and once again allow the men to chip away at the walls. Odelia wondered if they might all die from lack of nourishment before they made it out of the cave.

With gradual progress, the group made their way through the restrictive cave in a similar manner the rest of the night, their painstaking slowness causing knots of anxiety in Odelia's middle to cinch tighter with each stop. The whines of the children from the back of the line echoed in her ears, as did the immas quieting them.

When they reached the place where trickles of water ran from the heights of the tunnel beneath the Gihon Spring, they pressed their dry tongues shamelessly against the wall, savoring the coolness of the water, earth, silt, and minerals in the backs of their throats.

Aden passed the message down the line that they should take care to keep quiet in this stretch of the journey. They were walking beneath the Babylonian army and, although their presence should not be detected, no one knew if, at this depth, a toddler's cries would be heard by the Babylonians sleeping on the grounds outside the city's walls.

They kept at their task, stopping often for the soldiers to chip away enough room for the ark to pass, careful to give enough breadth that the ark would not scrape against the sides of the tunnel. At one point—the point where Odelia nearly had to slip sideways through herself, they stopped for nearly two hours to allow the soldiers to widen the sides of the cave.

"The first split is up ahead," Odelia whispered to Aden.

"And you know which way to go?"

The doubt painting the edge of his tone seeped into her own confidence. But it wasn't this part of the tunnel of which she was uncertain. "Yes."

After more stopping and more chipping away with the soldiers' tools, they reached the divide. "We go right." Odelia moved in that direction, grateful she could be assured of this.

Aden followed without a word. The cave widened, and they enjoyed steady travel for a good while. When the tunnel curved, Odelia stopped again, gazing into the darkness ahead of her, trying to gauge her whereabouts.

She, Avigail, and Joash had dreamed of one day emerging from the tunnels, of finding the eastern sea or perhaps the ancient cities of Sodom and Gomorrah. If Shaphan knew her foolish and childish intentions, Odelia doubted he'd have appointed her a leader of this undertaking. But when they were children, their aim had always been east. The symbolism of what they'd been doing—going east to find the sea where no creature could live, where Yahweh had rained down sulfur on sinful cities, hadn't occurred to her until close to the time she'd reached womanhood. That was when she'd told Avigail she would no longer join in on their childish romps. That was when she'd sought the temple over the silly fantasy of finding adventure beneath the city.

Unthinkable that Adonai would use the foolish wandering of her youth now, to potentially spare His mercy seat from the invading army.

For the first time since she'd left Shaphan at the pool in the late hours of the night, the darkness before them threatened to swallow her. Her breaths turned laborious as images of a burning Sodom danced in front of her, drawing out her fear that she would fail them all on this journey.

"Odelia?"

Her hands trembled as the group waited behind her.

"What is it?" Aden asked.

She inhaled a shaky breath. "Lack of air, I think." It had been a long time since she'd visited the tunnel this far. What if she remembered incorrectly? Worse still, what if her childhood memories were wrong? They had only reached the Valley of Jehoshaphat once, after all, still a long way from the Salt Sea. Why would Shaphan place such a heavy burden on her shoulders?

If only the visions before her would vanish. How was she to keep putting one foot in front of the other with the images of fire and torment upon her?

"Would you like me to take the lamp and go ahead? You can direct me."

She nodded. "Yes. I think I should like that." She handed him her lamp, their fingers brushing. Though the contact was only a moment, the strength of his callused fingers instilled a sense of security. She was not alone.

You foolish girl, she chastised herself. The very ark of the covenant was but several paces behind her—the mercy seat of the El

Shaddai. And yet it took the physical touch of a man to reassure her? Where was her faith? Would it fail her now when she needed it most?

"There is a divide ahead." Aden raised the lamp above their heads.

"We are getting farther, perhaps even past the army." The commanding soldier directly behind them, Jehoahaz, raised his own lamp from where he stood behind Odelia. "Which way?"

She closed her eyes, knowing the way but sensing a need to check. "Please, just a moment."

Yamin. Right.

Yamin, yamin, smol, yamin, smol, smol.

She, Avigail, and Joash had made the words into a singsong rhythm they could remember in their sleep.

Yamin, yamin, smol, yamin, smol, smol.

Right, right, left, right, left, left.

And to return home—*smol, smol, yamin, smol, yamin, yamin.*

Only, she would likely never again need to remember the second rhythm—the rhythm of the way home.

"We must go right."

Jehoahaz nodded. After more stops and chiseling, during which the children were given bits of precious bread and cheese to keep them quiet within the bowels of the earth, they continued onward, speaking only now and again, cautious that they could still be directly beneath the Babylonian army.

They took two more turns, left and then right, Odelia praying fiercely that each turn led them closer to their intended destination. Long past the time when the familiar, gnawing pit of pain in her stomach became near unbearable and her legs and arms grew weak from holding them tense, Aden stopped short, craning his head around to speak past Odelia. "The cave has collapsed in front of us."

"What?" Odelia peered around his shoulder. How could this be? In all her years of traveling the caves, she'd never encountered a collapse.

But Aden did not exaggerate, for there in front of him, the cave abruptly ended. A pile of rubble and debris covered the way forward, a space the size of a small basket at the very top. Odelia's heart sank. How long would it take to clear the path? Was it even possible?

Behind her, Jehoahaz directed everyone to step back several paces. It took a few long moments for those in the back to receive the message and obey the order.

"Excuse me, Odelia. I am afraid we must crawl over you," Jehoahaz said.

"Oh!"

Odelia dropped her bag to the ground of the cave and ducked down, pressing herself against the wall to allow Jehoahaz and his men to step over her in what felt like an awkward, childish game. One of the men's sandals brushed her headscarf, knocking it from her head. She scurried to readjust it but not before she caught Aden staring at her against the glow of her lamp.

The moment passed quickly, and yet an intense heat moved through her body at the intimate moment as she moved to adjust her headscarf.

Aden cleared his throat and stood, lifting his lamp to give the soldiers aid. "What is your assessment?"

"We'll have to move the line farther back so we can chip away at the rubble and create a wide enough space to pass. This may be a good time for a rest. Please pass along the word."

Aden spoke to the priest behind them, whose arms were heavy with a bag of treasures from the temple. A couple of the priests shuffled around, transferring the poles and the weight of the ark to fresh shoulders. They placed the temple treasures on the ground with care. Though all were younger than fifty, their muscles must ache from carrying the weight of the precious metals. The faint scent of incense emanated from the robes of the priest closest to her. She turned toward Aden, breathing in the cedar-and-herb scent of him, noting it as already familiar and comforting.

"You had best rest as well," Aden said to her.

"What about you?"

"I will hold the lamp for them to work by."

Odelia lowered herself to the cramped cave floor, the cool earth pressing along her spine and her tunic-covered legs. She dug in her bag for her extra mantle and, once she retrieved it, draped it over her shoulders. Leaning against the rock, she recited first the Shema and then the prayer from the scroll of Numbers that Shaphan had spoken over her in the temple room.

Had it truly only been two days since that time? And how long had they been traveling? Certainly, it must be morning, although it was hard to tell without seeing the placement of the moon or witnessing the rise of the sun over the horizon.

Her eyes grew heavy as she sank into the familiar words she'd known since childhood, their meaning fresh and new with the events of the past hours.

Hear, O Israel...

She let the word *shema* roll over her. The prayer was the first prayer taught to Hebrew children and, if so blessed, was the last prayer to depart one's lips before death. The word itself implied so much more than hearing. She allowed the muffled echoes of the soldiers battering the rubble to fade into the recesses of her mind.

Shema. To soak up, like a cake might soak up the sweetness of honey.

To hear. To care. To respond. With heart, soul, and strength.

Odelia hoped that's what she was doing in responding to Shaphan's request. In responding to the hitch inside that begged her to show love for Adonai in deed. Much like what she wanted to do for Hashem when she found him sick at the city wall.

Yet were her motives pure? She had left her abba and imma, had perhaps violated the fifth holy commandment.

With that final troubling thought, she fell into a sleep filled with visions of Sodom and Gomorrah alongside shining golden arks and the dirtied white robes of priests. In her dreams, she tried desperately to scrub the robes clean in the Jordan River, but the vicious scouring with lye caused her hands to become raw and bloody, dirtying the robes further. In her dream, a great earthquake broke the ark of the covenant open.

She gasped, sitting upright, trying to take in her bearings.

Beside her, Aden and the soldiers stood still, waiting, peering up at the cave as if it were about to tumble atop them.

The earthquake had not been confined to her dreams.

CHAPTER SIX

Odelia held her breath, waiting for another rumble. Would they all be buried beneath a pile of rocks, suffocated with limestone and earth? From somewhere down the line, the hollow echo of a sobbing woman met her ears. She thought of Hashem and wished for the familiarity of his thin arms around her waist.

They had taken the ark from Yahweh's dwelling place. What audacity they possessed. True, Jeremiah was not opposed to the scheme, but neither did he assemble the undertaking. Had Shaphan heard wrongly from Adonai?

After several long moments, nothing more happened. No loud crash, no collapsing walls.

Jehoahaz looked at his peers and then to Aden and the priests behind Odelia. "The Babylonians must have broken through the wall. Perhaps if it fell, the tremor traveled to us."

Adonai's judgment, then, but perhaps not in the way Odelia had at first assumed. She pressed a hand to her chest, gulping in the cool cave air. Aden knelt beside her. "All is well."

She nodded, though she wanted to argue. All was most certainly not well. The Babylonians broke through the wall of their beloved city. They would ransack the temple, chase down the king and his royal court, loot their homes, perhaps torture and kidnap their families. And Odelia had done the unthinkable by abandoning her abba and imma. By joining this clandestine mission—something she was not even certain Yahweh would bless. Babylonians could be discovering the cave now, racing toward them, ready to hunt them down like a shepherd does a jackal.

Her chest pressed tight, her breaths became rapid. She closed her eyes, grasping for strength. She could not crumple before these people who looked to her as their guide out of these caves. She could not faint and be useless to them. She could not fail them.

May He make His face shine upon you and be gracious to you; may He turn His face toward you and give you peace...

She unearthed the memory of Shaphan's prayer from the yawling screams of her anxiety.

"Aden," she whispered, the word like the echo of a moth between them.

He again lowered himself beside her, his hand inches from her arm, just shy of touching the linen of her mantle. "You are safe," he said in a voice so low and tender it wrapped around her like a warm blanket.

"Do you think they will find the tunnel? We are moving slowly. They will be upon us in no time."

She hated her wavering voice—the very sound of weakness. He may have seen her all those times praying in the temple, but of what value were her prayers and her faith if they all failed her now, when she most needed the assurance of Adonai's presence?

By the light of her lamp, which was low on oil, she glimpsed the bob of his throat. "I am sure Shaphan did his best to cover our trail. Their minds will be on finding the king and what treasures are left in the temple. They have no way of knowing we escaped and will not think to look for us."

"Shaphan said Adonai told him he'd die before the Babylonians broke through into the city."

"If it is so, then may he be at rest with his fathers."

Better to think of Shaphan resting with his fathers than beaten or dragged to Babylon, his old limbs exhausted and brittle with fatigue. And yet what of his body? What of a proper burial?

A lump formed in her throat. She wished for ashes, that she might pour them over her head and rub them into her skin to express her grief. None of it made sense. Why would Adonai permit such suffering to His servant?

The sound of a rock being dislodged from its perch near the soldiers shattered the quiet of the tunnel. Jehoahaz signaled for Aden and Odelia to crawl through to the other side. "We need to measure the ark against this opening. You two scout out the tunnel farther down, see if there are any more obstacles. But not too far. No more than three hundred cubits or so."

Aden turned to her, questioning wordlessly if she had any objections.

She appreciated the consideration. Her abba never bothered to take her opinion or comfort into account. She thought of Abba promising her to Adino. Would the man bring her abba to the elders if he did not deliver Odelia as promised?

More likely, all of them would be preoccupied with the invasion. Perhaps they hadn't yet even noticed her absence.

Odelia nodded to Aden, signaling her consent to go forward in the tunnel. True, she had never been alone with a young man without a chaperone, much less a man who had seen her without her headscarf, but these were pressing circumstances. She must lay aside the normal rules of life and put the good of these people, and the Lord's mercy seat, ahead of her comfort and modesty.

Aden handed his lamp to a soldier and hoisted himself through the opening without trouble. She allowed the same soldier to assist her over the small pile of rubble, her sandaled foot twisting and sliding in the pieces of splintered rock. Aden reached for her hand, and she took it, his warm fingers steadying her as she climbed over the remaining pile of rocks to the other side.

The soldier, Omri, handed Aden the lamp. "Best refill it with oil before you start out."

Aden lowered the lamp away from the scattering of rocks and rubble and poured reserve oil into the filling hole. When he completed the task, he straightened. "Ready?"

Odelia tightened her shawl around herself. "Yes."

She followed Aden into the dark of the cave, the lights and voices of the soldiers fading behind them. Soon, save for the light of their small lamp, darkness enveloped them.

"Do you remember if there is another turn soon?"

"There is. We must veer left."

"I give you credit for braving these tunnels as a child. You were either very courageous or very stupid."

She released a nervous laugh. "Likely a bit of both. They feel longer this time."

"You were not stopping every few feet to allow soldiers to chip away at walls."

"That is true."

They continued walking, the silence almost friendly and not as uncomfortable as she would have expected. "Are you worried for your abba?"

By the light of the lamp, he shook his head. "No." Two more paces. "That is not entirely true. I am a little worried for him. Although the Babylonians will take kindly to him and Jeremiah. As far as their army is concerned, Jeremiah is on their side. He has been urging the people to surrender to them all these years. They should fare well in Babylon, as should my uncle. Much better than in King Zedekiah's courtyard prison, I should think."

They walked several more paces before he spoke again. "And what of you? Are you worried for your family?"

She swallowed, attempting to gain a foothold on her emotions before answering. "I am." She could not manage more.

"I will pray they are spared. That they will find their way among the exiled. That they will find old friends in Babylon and make a new home for themselves."

"That is what Jeremiah says, is it not? For the captives to make a home among the pagans?"

"Yes. For them to build houses and settle, plant gardens, and marry. For them to seek the peace and prosperity of their new neighbors, and that in doing so, it will also go well for our people."

"Adonai's instructions do not always make sense, do they?"

Aden laughed, and the sweet rumble echoed off the caves. "Rarely."

"Why do you think that is?"

"Why do I think that Yahweh does not bow to our expectations?"

She bit the inside of her cheek. "When you say it like that, I suppose I am the one who does not make sense."

Aden shrugged. "I cannot understand it all myself. But I think, in the end, He only wants our best. He only wants us to love Him."

"I have tried hard to love Him. To pray fervently at the temple and obey the authority of my parents. The latter I did not always find easy."

Again, Aden chuckled.

"I am glad you think me amusing."

"I find you more refreshing than amusing."

"As I already told you, my forthrightness has gotten me in trouble a time or two."

"I think Adonai values honesty. King David was certainly honest in the writing of his psalms, and the Lord did not rebuke him."

Odelia allowed that thought to sink into her mind. She searched her memory for the reading of the psalms. "That is true. What else do you believe is involved with loving Adonai?"

"What questions you have for a girl!"

"Am I not supposed to think because of my gender?"

"N-no, that is not it at all. It is that I have spoken of such things only to my abba and peers. I did not think girls were interested in talk of theology."

"Well, I most certainly am."

"I am assuming your abba never taught you to read?"

"Of course not. All I heard growing up was that training girls to read was as much use as training sheep to card their own wool. Useless."

Aden fell silent. "That seems a bit harsh."

She shrugged. "It is the way of things. I do not need to learn to read to weave baskets or bake bread or raise children or please a husband."

"I could teach you once we are settled if you like."

She fumbled over her own feet, splaying out a hand against the wall to catch herself. Had she heard correctly? "What did you say?"

He stopped, and turned so the light of the lamp burned between them, illuminating the earnestness in his eyes. "I said I could teach you to read."

She wet her lips and swallowed around her dry throat. "I would very much like that." All the moisture that had been leeched from her throat found its way to her eyes.

Aden would teach her to *read*.

True, scrolls were not a commonplace item, but if she could learn to read, then perhaps she might teach herself to write. She could copy words down on clay tablets or scraps of papyrus after hearing the Torah read. She could have them forever.

She shook her head, sensing her thoughts running amok. As lovely as reading would be, more pressing concerns lay ahead of them. Concerns like getting the ark of the covenant safely away from the Babylonians. It was not the fault of Adonai that His people had not kept their part of the covenant promise. Why should the ark be carried off to foreign lands, or worse, melted down to create household gods of the Babylonians? She could scarcely fathom the prospect.

"Here. The next break in the tunnel."

She knew which direction they must go, but still she peered around him to glimpse the familiar split in their path. "We must go left."

Aden held his lamp toward the tunnel to their left. "It looks clear. We should go back and report to Jehoahaz."

She nodded and pressed her back against the wall so that Aden might slip by to take the lead. Instead, he held his hand out. "Perhaps you would like to go first on the way back?"

He was an upright man. If Adino had the opportunity to walk by her in such close confines, he'd take it, brushing up against her in whatever brazen way he saw fit.

"Thank you." She took the lamp from Aden and began the return trek, grateful for the widening walls in several sections that would allow quicker progress for the ark. Despite the opportunity to move faster, she slowed her steps, anxious for more time with Aden. Once they reached the soldiers, they'd only find themselves left with more waiting, anyway.

"We should continue our conversation," Aden spoke from behind her.

"About reading?"

"No, about what is involved in loving Adonai."

He was kind to name it as a conversation, when she was the one who had asked the question of him. Could it be possible he valued her musings on the matter?

"I am anxious to hear your answer," she said.

"I should like to hear yours first."

She pressed her lips together then said, "Very well. I think loving Adonai is giving Him preference above ourselves. I think it is emulating His character—His compassion and graciousness. He says He is slow to anger and abounding in love and faithfulness and wanting to forgive."

"You know your Torah."

"Do not all Jewish children?"

"Knowing the words is one matter. Inscribing them on our hearts is another."

"To shema," she whispered.

"To shema."

They walked several more paces in comfortable silence before Odelia spoke. "And now it is your turn. You must tell me how you love Adonai."

"Such personal questions for only just meeting." Was that a smile she heard in his voice?

One corner of her mouth lifted. "If transporting the ark of the covenant beneath the city does not make room for true conversation, I am unsure what would." As soon as the words left her mouth, she fought the urge to clamp her fingers over her lips.

But he only laughed. "Again, Odelia, you speak truth. You are a delight."

Though she was sure he didn't mean anything by it, the words spread warmth up her chest. Couching the serious conversation in light banter helped to keep her mind off the many other thoughts that vied for precedence in her head.

"And?"

"And...that is a question I have in fact been struggling with as of late. I believe you are correct—that loving Adonai means extending His character to others. Compassion, grace, faithfulness—taking care of the alien and the widow, the poor and the orphan. Perhaps stepping into places we don't feel suited for."

Did he mean the priesthood? "What part do you struggle with?"

He chuckled. "Good for you that you find it all so easy."

She cringed. "No, I do not—I mean, I fail often. But what is it that you find difficult?"

"I have been deep in my scrolls and learning all my life. I confess I have often neglected the action part of shema."

"Surely your learning also honors Adonai?"

He was quiet for a moment. "How?"

"You are learning His words and will educate others. You have even offered to teach me to read—that speaks of your generous spirit. You will one day offer sacrifices for our people when you complete your training. And I am certain you will find many opportunities to help the alien in the coming days, considering we will all be as such."

"A great but sad truth."

"Let us both strive to love Adonai better in the time ahead. And surely with His presence among us, we will do better."

Again, Aden grew silent.

They were almost back to the soldiers. Their chipping away at the shale and rock traveled to them through the tunnel. "Please, speak your mind," she said.

"I suppose I am doubtful if Adonai's presence is contained in the ark at this moment."

She blinked. "I do not understand. Do you think His spirit has fled?"

"I—I do not know. I only know of what Jeremiah prophesies—that the coming covenant will not include the ark."

For what must have been the twentieth time that day, Odelia remembered Shaphan's prayer. She slowed and turned to face Aden. "Even if Yahweh has abandoned the ark, He has not abandoned us. He is with us, Aden. We must believe that or all is lost."

She didn't know where the confident words had found root in her spirit, but once out in the open, she knew them to be true. Thank Adonai for revealing them to her.

Aden stared at her, his mouth slightly open. He raised a hand to her face, then, seeming to think better of his actions, lowered it. "Thank you, Odelia. Thank you for reminding me of things that are of utmost importance."

She smiled. "And thank you for believing my words worth hearing."

CHAPTER SEVEN

Once the soldiers finally widened the tunnel enough for the ark to fit through the collapsed part of the cave, the bedraggled group walked to the next divide without having to stop. Odelia surmised they must be well past the Babylonian army that had set up camp outside the city walls. They must be below the Valley of Kidron, perhaps close to the Valley of Jehoshaphat.

She directed them left through the last two splits, and as they approached what she thought to be the tunnel opening, her heart picked up speed, racing like a deer being chased on a hunt. Would the tunnel entrance be unobstructed? And if so, would the Babylonians be waiting for them? What were their next steps? She thought of Hashem, at the back of the line with the other women and children. She'd been so intent on guiding the group through the tunnel that she hadn't inquired about what would come next.

What exactly did they plan to do in the open plains of the valley? What dangers awaited them, and how adept would a handful of soldiers be at protecting them against any rebels or enemy army that sought to take the temple treasures for themselves?

Was this indeed a fool's mission?

"We should reach the end of the cave soon." She hoped Aden or the soldiers behind her did not hear the tremor in her voice. Had she guided them correctly?

"You have led us well." Aden lifted his lamp higher, brightening the path in front of them. Still, no sign of a cave opening, no smudge of daylight.

She readjusted the bag on her shoulder, its leather hide cutting into her skin after the night and morning of walking. Next time they stopped, she would fashion a padding out of one of her shawls or the few strips of linen she'd brought.

"Where will we go?" she asked.

Aden gestured in the direction they were walking. "We will follow the river east, toward the Dead Sea. There is a village along the way where we hope to purchase supplies, if the Babylonians have not already pillaged it. We plan to end our journey a bit south of Jericho, on the west bank of the Jordan River. There are ancient caves that no one has given much attention to."

"Will we build a tabernacle for the ark as Moses did in the wilderness?"

Aden grew pensive. "We will pray and listen for Yahweh to guide us."

They continued walking, and a knot of dread began to grow in Odelia's chest. They should have been there by now. They should see light.

"Another split. Which way?" Aden held up his lamp.

Odelia's mouth grew dry. Six turns. There were no more. She had remembered their childhood rhyme correctly, hadn't she? The end of the tunnel should be here!

"What? What is it?" Aden asked.

"There should not be any more splits. We should have reached the end."

"Did we take a wrong turn?"

"No, I am sure we did not."

But was she? Perhaps she had remembered incorrectly. Perhaps she had led them astray. Shaphan had trusted her in this, and she had failed him. Now, they may spend the rest of their short days wandering around in these tunnels, doomed to death, the ark lost forever.

Aden turned toward her. "Do not fear. We will find our way out."

But how?

She barely comprehended what Aden said to Jehoahaz, her mind a muddled pit of despair. They would all despise her—Aden, who had respected her until now, the soldiers, the priests. She would be scorned for the short remainder of their days.

After a moment, Aden turned to her again. "Jehoahaz is consulting with the other soldiers and with the map. He is unsure if we should turn back at the last split or continue on."

"I am a fool."

"You have gotten us this far. Adonai will guide us the rest of the way."

She bit her lip, praying silently that Aden's words would indeed prove true.

A short while later, Jehoahaz spoke to Aden. "We will continue onward. Take this left. We feel we are close."

Odelia had never prayed so hard in her life. They simply must find a way to bring the ark out of danger.

But again, they walked too long. The children whimpered, and Odelia wanted to moan alongside them. Surely they were going around in circles at this point? They couldn't backtrack even if they wanted to.

"There!" Aden's upbeat voice caused her to peer around his solid body. Ahead, the smallest sliver of gorgeous light met her sensitive eyes.

"Thank Adonai!" Emotion burned the backs of her eyelids.

Jehoahaz cleared his throat. "We will take over from here."

The soldiers squeezed by her and Aden to assume the lead, which Odelia was more than happy to give.

As Jehoahaz and his men signaled for them to stand back from the cave opening so they could scout the area, fear mingled with a grief wider than the Nile. The enormity of her decision crashed down upon her. There was no reversing the order of things. She would never see her parents or Avigail or Shaphan again.

She sniffed and pressed her back to the cool wall of the cave, scanning the small opening of light at the end of the gradual incline. Jehoahaz and his men crept toward the opening, like lions on a hunt, crouched low and creeping stealthily forward. Odelia held her breath as they disappeared from the cave.

Aden squeezed her hand, and a foreign spark traveled up her arm. Her gaze flicked to his, and he reassured her with a smile that warmed her to the temperature of Imma's cooking kiln.

"Perhaps that last scare was to keep you humble," he mused.

The smile that tilted her mouth felt wonderful. "If that was Adonai's intent, He certainly accomplished it."

He dropped his hand, and she closed her eyes, whispering yet another plea for Yahweh to protect them. Surely He would. Surely, if not for their sake, then for the sake of His mercy seat.

After what seemed like an endless time, the shadows of Jehoahaz's men appeared at the lip of the tunnel. Odelia breathed again.

Jehoahaz and Omri walked briskly toward them, their mouths in serious, firm lines. Jehoahaz gave a sharp nod. "We see no one. We expect the Babylonian encampments are on the other side of the Kidron hills. Still, we must proceed with caution. We do not expect anyone but a few shepherds for miles, as the tunnel has not led us to a road. Realize this does not mean we are safe—stray Babylonian outposts could be behind any hill or down any gorge. We will gather at the edge of the wadi before we continue our journey."

Aden glanced at the priest, who was now behind them, whom Odelia recognized from her many trips to the temple. Eliashib was his name. "Let us continue," Aden said.

Jehoahaz pressed his lips together then said, "There is something else."

"Go on." Eliashib adjusted his large pack.

"The city is burning. We see the smoke in the distance. It will no doubt upset the women and children."

Flashes of her parents, scurrying for safety or trying to save their most precious belongings amid a looted city, filled Odelia's mind. What would Imma try to save? The secret *teraphim* she hid in the bottom cupboard of the kitchen? Or the alabaster bowl that had been in their family since the Exodus from Egypt? Or would there be no time to gather any of their belongings, only time to run or obey the orders of the invading army?

Her chest tightened, and she struggled to pull air into her lungs.

"It is good of you to prepare us." Aden's furrowed brow told Odelia that it wasn't only the women and children who would find themselves upset at the news. "Should we let the others know?"

"I think that would be wise," Odelia said while Eliashib also spoke.

"I do not see what good it would do."

Odelia dipped her head in deference to the priest. "I spoke too quickly. Forgive me." Perhaps Aden hadn't been speaking to her. She'd grown accustomed to their talks on the journey. But everything would change now.

Aden cleared his throat. Although Shaphan had appointed him a leader of the group, as a young man he would be expected to follow the wisdom of the elder priests. "In the end, it is your decision, Eliashib. But if there is to be mourning and wailing, it might be better done within the bowels of this cave rather than out in the open. It will be hard enough to see our beloved city ruined."

Eliashib gazed at the floor of the cave, strands of silver hair poking out on the sides of his headwrap. The hem of his beautiful robes did indeed bear the marks of dirt. "I see the wisdom in what you say. Let me confer with the other priests." He walked deeper into the cave to where four priests carried the ark and three others some of the temple treasures.

A moment later, he walked back to where they stood. "We agree it is best to tell the women and children. We have passed along the message and encouraged those who wish to express their mourning to do so in the cave as best they can. We will pause before continuing."

Though Odelia realized the practicality of such instruction, she also couldn't ignore the harsh unfairness. To have lost everything they had ever known and to be told when and how to mourn for it all.

Moments later, low, guttural sounds echoed through the tunnel to her ears, so haunting and sad they caused tears to leak out of her eyes.

After a long while, Jehoahaz spoke to Aden and Eliashib. "We must keep moving."

They nodded.

"We will check with the guards we posted. If it is safe, we will signal for you to follow." Jehoahaz gestured his men toward the entrance of the cave.

Odelia bit her lip and followed Aden toward the light, the priests not far behind. After the soldiers conducted a perusal of their surroundings, Jehoahaz waved Aden forward.

The cool, dank earth gave way to dry, hot light. Odelia squinted, the sunlight painful and nearly blinding her after so much time belowground. She and Aden moved forward to make room for the rest of their group.

The edge of the wadi lay cracked and dry. The river of Jehoshaphat had not seen rain for several long months. They meandered down into the wadi and surveyed their surroundings. Clumps of brown brush, brittle grass, and dirt spread throughout the landscape. Not a sign of life—simply dry, open land. Odelia's throat grew parched from the heat, a reminder that the meager water in her goatskin flask would not last much longer. Jehoahaz had mentioned a village where they would obtain supplies, but Odelia saw no signs of a community as far as the horizon reached.

A gasp from behind reminded her what she had yet to face. She stood rooted to the fractured ground of the wadi. If she didn't look, just kept moving forward, she wouldn't have the imprint of the burning city forever on her mind. Hadn't the Lord told Lot and his family not to look back at the destruction of Sodom and Gomorrah, as the result of His just anger on the evil of the city?

And now, should she not look back, keeping her eyes instead on the direction of the Dead Sea and the ancient cities of destruction? A low sob came from one of the women, and Odelia turned, immediately wishing she hadn't.

Though she couldn't make out the glistening limestone walls of the city, it was impossible to miss the billowing smoke rising into the cerulean sky. It surprised her with its black-and-gray immensity, the way it spoke of complete destruction.

Why would they burn the city so quickly? Did they not need time to gather up the exiles—Odelia's people who would serve the Babylonians as slaves?

Unless... She swallowed down her next thought. Were they trying to burn them out? She imagined her parents hiding from the invading army in their cellar, the bet she had lived in all her life smoking above them.

A strangled cry escaped her lips. She fell to her knees beside some of the other women, a respectful distance away from the ark, pleading with Adonai for the loved ones and city they'd left behind.

She lowered her covered head to the scorched earth and touched her nose to the dust. She thought of the temple, where she'd spent so much time, being ransacked by the enemy army. Her home being burned. Even the lovely palace, built with beautiful wood from the forests of Gilead and Lebanon, would be reduced to rubble. When a small arm curled around her waist, she jumped, and when she saw it was Hashem, she threw her arms around him.

She burrowed her face in his unruly hair. "I will miss him," he murmured.

It occurred to her that while she would mourn her entire family and the city of her people, Hashem was only mourning the one other person in the city who had cared for him, Shaphan.

"King David wrote that 'weeping may stay for the night, but rejoicing comes in the morning.' We will not weep forever, Hashem. Adonai has a way of healing our hearts."

Though she believed the words, her heart sobbed alongside the boy's. Then, without warning, he straightened and wiped away the wetness on his face with his sleeve. "Enough of these poxy tears. We have an important journey ahead of us, and we cannot afford to waste the little water in our bodies on crying."

Her mouth twitched at the boy's abrupt change in tone. Better for Hashem to be a fighter. Once they were settled and the full weight of all they'd lost spread its black cloak over them, they would mourn. Once the ark was safe. Once they were safe.

"Those are wise words." Odelia rose with the rest of the women gathering around Jehoahaz and Aden. In the light, she surveyed the disheveled, malnourished group. It was bigger than she'd realized. No doubt surveying them in the dark of night, huddled by the Siloam Pool, had skewed her count. There must be at least forty of them, more than half of them women and children.

Families found one another after being separated during the tunnel journey. Odelia shared the last of her rations with Hashem when a long-forgotten but familiar voice called to her from behind.

"Odelia! Is it truly you?"

CHAPTER EIGHT

"Sherah?"

The girl's exotic, dark eyes widened. "Praise Adonai, it is you!" The young woman flung her arms around Odelia and squeezed until Odelia thought she might have to beg for breath. "I am so happy to see you, my friend!"

Odelia closed her eyes, savoring the familiar embrace. True, the girls had not been close friends since they were children. The sprouting of womanhood had served to sever them, as Sherah had matured much earlier than Odelia, her curves and striking features calling her to a different set of friends. While Odelia sought time in the temple, Sherah sought out friends who held the same interests as her—interests involving the opposite gender. And although Odelia had tried not to be hurt when she glimpsed her childhood friend giggling with Avigail on her cousin's rooftop, she never quite healed from the hurt of rejection.

But now, there was no denying that preserving any part of her former life, even the painful parts, was a treasure. "I did not see you by the pool last night," Odelia said.

"I was late as usual. I caught up with the group before Shaphan closed the tunnel."

So the dear priest had ordered the tunnel hidden—likely one of his last acts of service to Adonai. To her and Aden and Hashem and all who traveled with them.

"How did you come to be here?"

Something shifted between them, and Odelia regretted her question, hoping Sherah didn't think her presuming airs.

"I mean, I did not know—I thought..." *You would cling to your Asherah pole until the Babylonians pried you from it with their hot, meaty hands?* There was no dignified way to finish the sentence out loud.

Sherah tossed her headscarf over one shoulder, and Odelia noted the bony protrusion of her dusty cheekbones, the wet trail along their smoothness, a reminder that the Babylonians had starved them all. That whoever was left would have little strength to fight enemy invaders. "Jehoahaz is my brother."

Odelia glanced at the rugged commanding soldier. Yes, she knew Sherah had an older brother named Jehoahaz, of course, but he'd been away training for most of the time they'd been romping about as children. "Oh, that is wonderful. And what of your parents?" She craned her head to see if she could glimpse the kind, familiar faces of her friend's abba and imma. Scurrying into Sherah's house for a honey or date cake from the kitchen of Sherah's imma had been a high point of Odelia's childhood.

Sherah lowered her gaze to the ground. "Abba succumbed to the paralysis last month. One side of his body is useless. He could not make the journey, and Imma would not leave him."

Odelia's hand fluttered to her throat. "Sherah, I am so sorry."

"We all left something—or someone—we love behind." Sherah placed her hand on Odelia's arm, the bangles at her bone-thin wrist jingling. "What of your parents?"

Odelia licked her lips. "They too are in the city." It was not a lie. Neither was it the entire truth. For what words could she speak that would not implicate her as a traitor to her family?

Sherah again wrapped her in a hug. "We will grieve together. All of us."

Odelia squeezed her childhood friend, the scent of incense wafting gently to her nose. When they began to part, Sherah turned to the young woman beside her, gesturing to her as she looked at Odelia. "Do you know Zillah? She is trained in the art of healing and midwifery. Jehoahaz asked Shaphan if she might come along." Sherah leaned in closer to Odelia and Zillah. "My brother thinks Zillah hung the moon and the stars. The ink on their betrothal contract was still wet when we heard of the plans to escape."

Zillah smiled and dipped her head. The girl nearly matched Sherah's brother in height. The two would have wonderfully tall children. Odelia tried to think of a wedding celebration in their new home, wherever that might be. Without Sherah's parents. Without Shaphan and her own parents.

Sherah slipped her arm into Odelia's. "Do not look so glum, dear friend. The ark will protect us for the remainder of our journey. We will grieve, yes. But we will soon find food, and we will also rejoice because we are those who have been saved from the Babylonians."

Odelia winced. She wasn't ready to rejoice yet. And Sherah's words troubled her. For Jeremiah had rebuked the people for putting their trust in the temple instead of in Yahweh. What, then, was the difference in transferring that trust to a block of acacia wood gilded in gold?

She squeezed her eyes shut, silently begging Adonai's forgiveness. Why would He choose her for a charge such as this one when her heart was so quick to wrestle with Him over His ways?

She introduced Hashem to Sherah and Zillah, the boy appropriately mortified at their fawning over his adorable foreign looks. And when Sherah kept her arm slipped in Odelia's and pulled her forward, she savored the oft-unknown feeling of being wanted. "Will you walk with us, Odelia?"

She searched for Aden but did not see him in the crowd. He likely had no need of her now that they had exited the caves. It would be more appropriate if she stayed with the rest of the women and children. "I would like that."

After the priests and soldiers conferred, Jehoahaz climbed up the bank of the wadi to address them. The leather sheath of his sword hung at one side, his arrows on the other. He clutched his bow with his hand and looked across the craggy terrain. A single olive tree stood at the top of the wadi, and a pair of young boys sat under it, gathering pebbles for their slings.

"Everyone is tired, hungry, and thirsty, but it is not yet safe to stop, and we will not be able to gather the supplies we need. We must continue until dusk. When we make camp, some of my men will travel north to obtain supplies. We will keep to the wadi. My men will survey the top of the ravine. You are safe under their watch."

One of the priests said a prayer over them. Hashem gestured to the two boys who had sat beneath the olive tree, and Odelia nodded. Of course he would want to be with his peers.

Sherah sipped the last of her water from a pouch hanging from her belt. "How do you know the boy?"

"I found him near the city gates several years ago. He was sick and alone."

Sherah wrinkled her nose. "I am surprised your abba allowed you to take him in, even if he is a cute pet."

Odelia cleared her throat. "He did not, though Shaphan often cared for him."

Sherah sobered at the name of the older priest. "Shaphan always held a soft heart toward the outcasts among us. If only he felt the same for his own people."

Odelia straightened, her spine as rigid as iron. "What do you mean?"

Sherah waved her bangled wrist through the air. Their pace was painstakingly slow, and yet they were weak with hunger and could only go as fast as the slowest in their group. "Forgive me, Odelia. I forgot he treated you like kin. Shaphan had his favorites, no doubt."

"Could we stop referring to him as if he were dead and gone?" Even though the older priest himself had been certain of his death before the Babylonians broke through Jerusalem's walls, Odelia refused to think of his unburied body lying in Jerusalem's looted streets or alone in his small bed.

"My, you are prickly about him, are you not? Very well. You might as well know that Shaphan did not approve of my betrothal to Malachi. When my abba asked his opinion on the union, the old dog didn't bite his tongue on his thoughts. He is the reason I am not married this day. He is the reason I will never see Malachi again."

Odelia's bottom lip quivered. She did remember seeing Malachi at the market with Sherah before Passover. The young man held the confident swagger of a young King David. While all the girls had been tripping over their tunics for his attention, he seemed all too willing to give each of Odelia's peers their due, flirting shamelessly with one girl and getting her hopes up that he might approach her abba before moving on to another love interest.

Odelia understood the counsel Shaphan had given Sherah's abba, and she respected the man for it.

"I am sorry about Malachi."

"Thank you," Sherah spoke softly and then sighed. "I suppose Zillah will be the only one of us to marry out in this wilderness."

Zillah giggled. "I see some handsome friends of your brother's."

Sherah narrowed her eyes. "They are handsome, but military duties have taken my brother away so much. I think I should like someone with a more scholarly air."

"I am afraid to tell you, my friend, but if you could not find a scholar when you lived in the City of David, I am not certain you will find one out here in the desert." Zillah pulled her head covering down to shade her face from the blinding sun.

"Oh, I may yet find favor with Adonai. Did you see the young man conferring with the priests? The one carrying the earthenware jar and the leather cylinder?"

Odelia's heart seized. Aden. Should she speak up? Perhaps tell Sherah that Aden had shown interest in *her*. But had he? More than likely, he was simply being nice.

Odelia sighed. If her friend set her sights on Aden, then no doubt, he would succumb to her charm. Sherah was beautiful. Even in a malnourished state, she boasted an abundance of curves Odelia could never hope to have even when hale and hearty.

"I did see him," Zillah said. "Do you know who he is? Perhaps he is training to be a priest?"

Odelia kept her head low as she walked onward. Familiar cramps burned her legs. The pains had started when their rations had been severely cut, about nine months ago when their stores had greatly diminished. While their intensity came and went, they never entirely disappeared. "He is."

She couldn't tamp down the bit of pride she felt at the information she shared.

Sherah's head snapped up. "How do you know him?"

"The prophet Jeremiah's scribe adopted him into his house as a babe. His blood, however, is priestly. He will be trained as such."

"You are avoiding the question, my friend." A cutting edge fringed Sherah's teasing tone.

"We walked in the tunnel together. Shaphan introduced us." No need to volunteer her part in leading the group through the tunnels. It would only sound like boasting. And no need to boast when she had nearly gotten them all lost in the bowels of the earth.

Sherah released a humorless chuckle. "It appears our Shaphan cannot give up his matchmaking habits, even when he knows he will not see the results. Although I for one am glad he no longer has a say in whom I marry." Sherah sniffed. "But neither will Abba or Imma. They have given me the last of their talents in hopes it will serve as a dowry, but who will manage such things? Am I to arrange them myself?"

Why were any of them daydreaming of marriage in a time such as this? Did they not have greater worries in transporting the ark to its new home, in surviving the journey and escaping rebel armies, in avoiding dying from hunger and thirst?

And yet, the reality was that they were single maidens. They had spent their lives beneath the roofs of their abbas, never expecting to be on their own. Always, a man would provide for their safety. But now? Now, this small community had no other purpose than to save the temple treasures. To survive.

"I cannot help but be curious, Odelia. What is your assessment of the young man…?"

"Aden," Odelia ground out, already regretting agreeing to walk with the two women.

"What is your assessment of *Aden*?"

"Sherah…" Zillah admonished her friend.

Sherah whirled on Zillah. "Do you not wish to know? If I am now in charge of my own dowry and interested in pursuing a husband, I need to be careful not to step on the sandals of an old friend." She smiled at Odelia. "If you have set your sights on him, I will look for another."

"I think we should not be anxious over finding husbands until the ark is safe and we are fed."

"Can I assume that you do not care for this man?"

"I hardly know him. Though what I have seen is honorable, and Shaphan regarded him highly."

Sherah rolled her eyes. "That hardly sounds like love."

Odelia studied the hem of her dusty tunic as she walked on the broken earth. "I never expected love would be an option for me."

Sherah straightened. "So if I flirt a bit with him, you will not mind?"

"She did not say that, Sherah." Zillah raised her eyes to the heavens, part in mock frustration, part in amusement.

"She is not saying much of value, is she?" Sherah softened the words by jostling Odelia in the shoulder with her own. "But you are correct about one thing. We need not worry about marriage if we die of hunger before we have a chance to catch husbands. Oh, how I miss Imma's raisin cakes!" At the name of her beloved imma, Sherah began to sob.

Zillah patted her friend's shoulder while Odelia looked helplessly on, holding out a hand to the sleeve of Sherah's mantle but stopping short of touching the fabric.

"There, there," Zillah crooned. "None of our bodies can afford to waste our tears. I am surprised you have any left, my friend."

Sherah swiped at the corner of her eye with her sleeve. "You are right. Thank you, Zillah. We must stay together. You too, Odelia. As far as I can see, we are the only single women here. If we cannot depend on our abbas or husbands to look after us, then we must look after one another. We must make our own covenant."

"I agree," said Zillah. "Although I do believe your brother will guard us with his life, he will no doubt be occupied with the affairs of the entire group."

Odelia bit her lip. Jeremiah had spent the reign of the last five kings berating her people for the poor job they had done of keeping Yahweh's covenant. Did she have any right to make another with two women she barely knew?

Still, Sherah was right. Going through the tunnel with Aden, Shaphan's words and prayer still fresh in her mind, she'd not felt quite as alone. But here, out in the wilderness, with Shaphan back in that burning city, with her abba and imma either dead or forced into exile, and with Aden up front with the soldiers and priests occupied with more important things than the small, plain girl who prayed often at the temple, she realized she had no one to depend on.

"Odelia?" Sherah raised hopeful eyes in her direction.

"The boy. I have an obligation to Hashem as well."

"Of course," Zillah said.

But Sherah narrowed her gaze at Odelia. "The Gentile boy?"

"Shaphan circumcised him. He has accepted our ways with all his heart. He is one of us as surely as the priests are."

Sherah's eyes widened. "A single circumcision and you dare compare him to a priest?"

"I mean to say his heart is pure." She thought of the priests Jeremiah spoke against—priests such as her abba. Perhaps comparing Hashem to the priests was not entirely accurate, for in many ways Hashem's heart surpassed the purity of some of Adonai's elect.

"Of course, we will watch out for him." Zillah searched for the boy a couple of groups ahead of them. "He is an orphan as are we."

Her words weighed heavy, their truth winding around them, binding them tighter together, whether they chose the bond or not.

"Thank you," Odelia said.

Sherah shrugged. "He looks capable enough. Who knows? He may prove helpful to us in the end."

Odelia stopped herself from rolling her eyes heavenward. She had not chosen who Adonai sent on this journey, but she would see that Hashem was not abused by these women.

"It is settled then." Zillah gave a firm nod. She looked behind them, where the next group, consisting of young immas and small children, traveled several paces from them. She reached for first Sherah's hand, and then Odelia's. "With this covenant and under *Adonai El Elyon*, we are sisters and family. We will no longer be orphans. We will seek the good of each other and, with Yahweh's blessings, we will find peace and thrive in our new home."

Sherah squeezed her hand. "We are sisters now."

Though Odelia had never participated in such an oath, she couldn't deny the comfort of it. A vow under the Lord Most High God. She needn't see eye to eye with these women on every subject under the sun. But they vowed faithfulness and love. With them, she would belong.

And that is what she needed now, more than ever.

CHAPTER NINE

"What do you think he is saying?" Zillah asked.

Odelia eyed the pair of men Jehoahaz spoke with—the only strangers they'd come upon. The men's eyes shone wide at the obvious contents carried by the priests. Now, Jehoahaz spoke to the strangers with bright eyes and a lot of intense gesturing.

Sherah retied her headscarf. "He is likely instructing them not to say anything about what they have seen. The safety of the ark may depend upon their silence."

She was right. What audacity they possessed to parade the temple treasures out in the open, thinking they could deliver them to safety! But surely Adonai would make it possible.

The two strangers parted amicably, and the group resumed their slow, plodding procession. Some of the children and women in the back trailed behind, causing their almost sluggish speed. When Jehoahaz finally signaled them to make camp for the night, the entire group released a collective sigh. The soldiers ordered them to gather what dry sticks and brambles they could find along the wadi to make a fire. Once several small fires crackled, Odelia lowered herself to the cold ground, Sherah and Zillah on either side of her. She would check on Hashem soon, but her burning legs needed just a moment...

"We are going to sleep out in the open?" Sherah wrapped her arms around her legs, a visible shiver working through her body.

"I do not see any caves in the area. They must still be worried about having to pack quickly. If we need to hide or leave in a hurry, it would be a severe loss to leave the tents behind." Odelia gazed up at the star-studded sky, sinking into the comfort that the vast array twinkling down upon them provided.

Sherah curled on the ground, using her goatskin bag as a pillow. "I am so hungry," she moaned.

Odelia bit her lip, digging in her bag for the last bit of bread she'd taken from her home that morning. She broke it in four, handing a meager slice to first Zillah and then Sherah. She tore off a small corner of the piece that was left for herself before storing the rest in her bag for Hashem.

"That is kind of you, Odelia. Thank you." Zillah tore off the tiniest portion of bread with her teeth, chewing carefully. "I have seven roasted pistachios I will share with you both tomorrow."

Sherah laughed. "How pathetic that I will likely be dreaming about my portion of those pistachios the entire night."

Zillah giggled. "You waste your dreams on nuts? Mine are filled with honey cakes."

"I have dreamed of meat—any kind of meat—for the last several months. Venison, goat, lamb…oh, roast mutton would be divine." Odelia's mouth watered.

"Did I hear you say mutton?" Across from her, Hashem settled himself by the fire. His knobby knees poked out from beneath his too-small tunic.

"Just dreaming." Odelia handed him the portion of bread. "Did you find some new friends today?" Although he bore the marks of hunger as they all did, he appeared more content here, under the stars, outside the city walls.

"I think so. They did not cast me off as a Gentile when they found out how handy I was with a sling."

Odelia raised an eyebrow. "I hope you were not slinging rocks too close to the group, Hashem." She winced. "Or too close to the ark or the priests."

The flames of the fire lit up a mischievous grin on the boy's dark features. "I only skimmed one of the priests' headwraps. He hardly noticed."

"Hashem!" She burrowed her face in her hands while Sherah nearly rolled on the ground with laughter.

"And I was worried he would be a burden. I think I am going to enjoy having this one around, Odelia."

Hashem puffed out his chest. "You will quite enjoy it once I become the first one to kill a wild goat with my sling."

Zillah groaned. "No more talk of food! I cannot bear it."

Odelia formally introduced the two women to the boy. The wife of one of the priests came to their fire to offer a skin of barley beer. "Shalom. I am Eliana, wife of Oren."

Odelia held out her flask for Eliana to pour a small amount into. "Shalom and thank you. My name is Odelia. May I help you?"

Eliana switched the skin to her opposite hip and smiled. Odelia guessed Eliana to be ten years older than her, with uncommon light skin and a severe dimple in one cheek.

Eliana shook her head. "You are my last group. I am going to rest now, but it was good to meet you."

"Odelia."

Odelia whirled at the sound of her name, blood rushing to her limbs at the sight of Aden walking toward her, something like relief on his handsome face.

"I am glad to see you are well."

She dipped her head. "Of course. I thought it more appropriate I travel with the women and children now that my purpose for our journey is complete."

Aden nodded, a smile twitching his lips. "But I have missed the conversation you provide. I am afraid the priests are not half as amusing."

Her mouth fell open, but as she grappled for a suitable response, Sherah pushed in beside her. "Shalom," she said to Aden. "I am Sherah. Would you like to sit for a moment? I have some bread and a bit of beer."

She had bread, did she? Odelia gathered a breath and swallowed, acknowledging that hunger and fatigue made her increasingly irritable.

Aden flashed Sherah an easy smile. "I must return to my post." He met Odelia's gaze. "I only thought to be certain you are settled."

She couldn't comprehend the look in his piercing eyes, nor how he acted as if one of the most beautiful women in Judah wasn't drooling at his feet this very moment. "Thank you."

"Do the soldiers need help?" Hashem sidled up to Aden. "I know my way around a sling."

Aden sized up the boy. "Yes, I think I noticed that earlier in the day when you were playing target practice with Oren's turban."

Appropriately chastened, Hashem's face grew visibly red even by the scant light of the fire. "Elias dared me—" He stopped short. "I will not do it again. I promise."

Aden ruffled the boy's hair, and Hashem seemed to grow three inches beneath the male attention. "See to it. Perhaps when we are settled you can show me your skills with a sling on a more suitable target?"

"I would like that very much."

Aden gave one more quick smile to Odelia before walking off. She watched the back of him, how he checked on each group, making friendly conversation, how he seemed so completely at ease despite the harrowing circumstances of their day—despite the insurmountable journey ahead of them.

"I think he might be even more handsome up close." Zillah looked after Aden's retreating back. "And you seem to have his attention, Odelia."

Odelia added some dried dung a soldier had handed out earlier to the fading coals.

Sherah shifted her eyes from Aden back to her two companions. "He is an honorable man, is all. She ran off without telling him where she was going. Of course he would want to know her whereabouts." She brushed invisible dirt off the arm of her tunic. "What purpose did you speak of?"

Odelia pretended not to hear the question.

"Odelia? What purpose did you have?"

Hashem spoke from where he lay on the dirt. "Odelia knows the underground tunnels better than anyone in all Jerusalem. She is the one who guided us out of the city!"

Odelia's skin warmed. "I used to play in the caves when I was a girl. Shaphan thought I could be of some use." She couldn't bring herself to volunteer how she'd almost gotten them all lost.

Sherah raised an eyebrow. "*You* used to run amok beneath the city? My, you are full of surprises, are you not?"

"It was a game I played with my cousins. Silly, really. And quite dangerous. Almost as irresponsible as using a priest's holy head-wrap for target practice."

Hashem blushed again as he readjusted his pack to use as a pillow.

Zillah inched closer to the fire, curling in a ball on the dirt. "I suppose it is good for us that you played such an irresponsible game with your cousins as a child. I never would have been able to pick through the twists and turns of that horrid tunnel. If I never see a cave as long as I live, it will be too soon."

Odelia hadn't the heart to tell her that they chose their intended destination for its abundance of caves.

They grew quiet, the crackling of the fires and low voices the only sounds cutting through the cold night. In the distance, the flicker of torches guarded their camp, keeping away jackals, wolves, and hyenas. Odelia whispered the Shema over their small group.

She wondered how the ark would fare out in the open or if the priests had set up a dwelling for it. Imagine, the very presence of Adonai, the Shekinah glory, seated upon the throne of the ark only a short distance from her. And yet, should she feel different so near

His glory? Bolder, more faithful, more trusting? Was Yahweh's presence in that manmade holy box or had He fled them?

She closed her eyes. She might never know the answers to her questions. Why her parents never truly seemed to want her, why she wasn't enough. Why Adonai had given her the hard choice of leaving them for this journey—a journey that may very well end in failure. And if Adonai's presence had already fled the ark, what did any of it matter?

She fell asleep with the questions whirling in her head. Visions of fire filled her dreams along with hazy forms of Abba and Imma. Of Sodom and Gomorrah. Of bloodied priestly garments. Of a beautiful light shining upon the ark. Of the earthenware jar Aden carried. Of Jeremiah's scroll.

When she awoke, she felt no more rested than when she had fallen asleep.

Odelia lay still in the quiet morning, listening to the muted sounds of a babe crying amid hushed voices. The scent of the fire's dying coals lingered in the air.

Beside her, Sherah stretched and groaned. No, *moaned*, was a more accurate description. "Every inch of my body hurts."

Zillah answered Sherah's complaint with a muffled lament of her own. "I feel like I slept on the points of a hundred swords."

Odelia lifted her aching body off the dirt floor of the ravine inch by painful inch. Not that any of them were accustomed to the fine feather beds of kings and queens, but hunger had a way of causing constant pain, of poking slight annoyances and discomforts until they turned into the intensity of growling lions.

Sherah threw an arm over her head. "As much as I am hurting, I fear getting up will be even more painful. Has the contingent of soldiers found supplies?"

Odelia stretched her neck. "They were to travel by the light of the moon to a village north of here. But the gates will not open until dawn. I wonder if they will ask us to keep walking until then."

Sherah moaned again, then to Odelia's horror, began sobbing. "May Adonai let me die if I have to walk another step without food!"

Zillah's lips pulled downward, and she patted her friend's back. "We are going to live, Sherah. We must not despair. Besides, I have the pistachios I promised."

Sherah nodded, her bottom lip still trembling. How did the girl look attractive even with protruding bones and a face washed in tears?

Across from the smoking fire, Hashem rubbed his eyes. "Waking up to a sobbing woman is worse than being awakened by a pack of hungry hyenas."

Sherah glared at the boy. "Perhaps you and your friends would like to go find some."

Hashem stood and stretched his arms overhead. "Hyena meat is very gamey, not to mention unclean. But if I do find some, I will send them your way."

Zillah hid a giggle in the sleeve of her shawl, but Sherah scooped up a palm of dusty rocks and flung them in Hashem's direction.

Hashem shook his head. "Linus was right about one thing—women do not make sense. Yesterday you were happy to have me around. Today you are raining curses on me." He began to walk away but stopped short to wave at Odelia. "Shalom, Odelia."

"Shalom," she whispered.

Zillah clucked her tongue, or at least tried to but seemed to find the roof of her mouth too dry. "Come now, Sherah. We are all suffering. You need not take it out on the boy."

"I know!" Sherah wailed, this time with no tears coming from her sobs.

"Here." Zillah dug in her bag for the promised pistachios and doled out two for each of them. "I will save the remaining one for our feisty friend if he returns. Perhaps Sherah can give it to him as a peace offering."

But Sherah ignored her friend as she broke open the pistachio, chewing it with the utmost care. When they'd eaten the nuts, they stuck their tongues inside the shells, trying to get every last bit of flavor and nutrients from the casing. Sherah gave up and popped the shell in her mouth, eliciting a great crunch.

The soldiers signaled for them to pack their belongings and scatter the evidence of their fires. It was the month of *Tammuz*, and the sun shone before them in a ball of red, slowing them even more than the day before.

If the Babylonians, or any enemies, came upon them, they would not stand a chance of running or fighting. Each step proved slow and painful, and Odelia began to grow nauseated in the heat.

From somewhere in the front, one of the priests began reciting from the scroll of Jeremiah, and the group repeated each line until it could be heard from the back. At first, the words were those of warning and judgment. About Adonai's people forsaking Him, the

Spring of Living Water, and trading Him in for broken cisterns of their own making. About the houses and the palace of Jerusalem being filled with dead bodies at the hands of the Babylonians. Yahweh Himself would hide His face from the city that had committed such wickedness.

Odelia pushed on. At one point, Sherah leaned against her for support, and it was all she could do to hold up the girl along with her own weight.

They didn't pass any travelers. Odelia wondered if the outlying towns had already been taken over by the invading army and brought into exile, if they hunkered down in their villages or had perhaps run to the mountains to hide.

Why hadn't they listened to Jeremiah? For decades he'd been forecasting the demise of the city, but the king and leaders and even most of the priests had cast him off as a heretic and false prophet. How wrong they'd been.

Just when she was tempted to give into despair, though, the words from the priest changed in tone. Like a cool splash of fresh water, the words from the scroll revived her spirit.

"'Nevertheless, I will bring health and healing to it; I will heal my people and let them enjoy abundant peace and security.'"

Odelia clung to the words as if they were water and manna.

"'I will cleanse them from all the sin they have committed against Me and will forgive all their sins of rebellion against Me.'"

Hope wound around her as she whispered the words past cracked, dry lips.

"'Then this city will bring Me renown, joy, praise, and honor before all nations on earth that hear of all the good things I do for it;

and they will be in awe and will tremble at the abundant prosperity and peace I provide for it.'"

Quick, rasping breaths of emotion constricted her lungs. Such beautiful words, but would she live to see such a day? Seventy years Jeremiah said they'd be in captivity. If she lived long enough, she'd be an old lady by the time she returned to the land of her people. Could she live on the simple hope of Yahweh's words and promises until then?

CHAPTER TEN

The words of Jeremiah's scroll had long since passed their lips when a billowing cloud of dust appeared to the north. Odelia raised a hand to shield her eyes from the sun. Was she seeing a mirage, or was it the Babylonians? Or maybe a post of Assyrians come to steal the temple treasures?

The priests slowed, and the soldiers scanned the area, seeming to decide whether to take cover among the brambles or stand and protect the ark. But then Jehoahaz's voice rang out, loud and joyful. "It is our men! With supplies!"

Sherah crumbled to the ground, sobbing a prayer of gratitude. Zillah and Odelia fell beside her, doing the same. "Thank you, Adonai," Odelia whispered. "You have heard our prayers. You will bring us healing and health and peace and security because you are merciful."

As the soldiers grew closer, Odelia took in the sight. In the lead were several donkeys loaded with baskets of grain, jugs of oil, food supplies, and *minas* of wool atop creaking oxcarts. A dozen goats and sheep and lambs—some too skinny to possess much meat on their bones—followed the oxcarts. The temple treasury must have provided well, thank Adonai.

"We will rest for the remainder of the day and night. Set up your tents, gather with your families. Let no one eat until we have offered the first sacrifice to Yahweh." Jehoahaz conferred with Eliashib as he spoke. Would the priest take the role of the new high priest now that the other had stayed behind?

They moved onto a plain on the side of the wadi and the priests, soldiers, and men pitched a tent for the ark to rest. The women started fires and began heating up the cooked chicken the soldiers had purchased. The priests who had brought lyres and harps played and sang the psalms of David before the ark. The children Hashem's age and older assembled the goat-hair tents.

As the odor of the food permeated the dry air, Odelia thought she would again be sick. She sipped the last of the warm barley beer from her flask, and it managed to quell the sour bile rising in her stomach.

She crouched by the heat of their fire, holding a long stick stuck through the body of the chicken. Odelia held one end and Zillah the other, when she caught her new friend's mouth hanging open.

Keeping a firm grasp on the stick, Odelia turned, her own jaw dropping at the sight before her, a couple of hundred cubits off. There, the priests and soldiers had erected the unmistakable sight of the tabernacle.

The elaborate tent, about ten cubits by thirty cubits long, was covered in goat skins and smooth leather, the multiple coverings concealing the inside, where Odelia assumed the ark now rested. For the sake of the priests who had been carrying it on their shoulders all this way, she was grateful.

"It must be the very same tabernacle from the days of the wilderness, don't you think?" Zillah wiggled the stick that speared the chicken, signaling for Odelia to lift her end lest it droop into the fire.

"It must have been stored in the temple. We—we have returned the ark of the covenant to its original home."

"We are back in the wilderness." Sherah tore a piece of bread in two, rationing out pieces for herself, Odelia, Zillah, and Hashem. Odelia knew it took all of Sherah's will not to shove some in her mouth before the trumpet sounded and the official sacrifice was made—as much will as it took Odelia not to tear off a piece of juicy roasted chicken beginning to pop and sizzle in the heat of the fire.

Odelia thought of the promises of Adonai revealed in the scrolls of Jeremiah. "If we are back in the wilderness, perhaps we will once again cling to Yahweh's promises." Cling to Him. "Maybe that is how He wants it."

Sherah tore a piece of bread especially hard. "Seems Adonai cannot ever get enough glory for Himself," she pouted.

"Sherah!" Zillah hissed.

"It is true. And now here we are, back in the desert, praying for manna, and once again the ark is hidden from our eyes."

Unexpected rage bubbled up within Odelia. Not simply at Sherah's callous words, but at her constant complaining and grumbling. Her childhood friend expected Odelia to bear her weight during their walk. She treated Hashem poorly. Now, she sat away from the intense heat of the fire, making herself available for only the simplest task.

"Would you rather be back in that burning city? Or perhaps a slave in Babylon? We have food here. And how dare you speak of Adonai with such disrespect—you, with your time at the Asherah poles, with your worship of Ba'al and the queen of heaven. Do not look surprised—of course I know your faithlessness. I simply cannot understand why Adonai has not yet struck you dead for your complaining!"

As soon as the words left her mouth, Odelia knew she'd spoken out of the blackness of her own heart. A blackness as deep as that of an onyx stone. If she could have simply dropped the chicken in the fire, she would have turned and fled. Zillah sat still as stone, staring into the flames.

Sherah glared at Odelia then stood. "I should have never invited you to walk with us. You are a wretched sister." She stomped away, leaving Odelia and Zillah to turn the chicken silently over the flames.

After a moment, Odelia groaned. "I should not have said such things."

Zillah didn't speak at first. Finally, she opened her mouth, her words coming slowly.

"You are right in saying Sherah has not been faithful to Adonai, but which one of us has? Is that not why we need His presence with us, why we are on this journey? Even King David told Adonai the truth of his feelings. Perhaps, in Sherah's own way, she is doing the same."

Her friend's words did nothing to alleviate Odelia's pain.

Zillah continued. "I know she can be difficult. I think…how she left her abba and imma was very painful for her."

"We have all lost those dear to us." Odelia didn't bother to stomp out the bitterness creeping into her tone. Yet could she pretend that her loss was the same as her friend's? Sherah's parents had adored her, and each other, and had never bothered to hide that fact. If anything, Odelia often felt like a stranger in her own family.

And yet, loss was loss. Grief was grief. Who could compare?

"I know, Odelia. I know."

They continued turning the chicken until the priest blew the trumpet, signaling that they should gather at the tabernacle for the offering of the sacrificial lamb, as well as for the liquid and grain offerings. They did so, and before their makeshift tabernacle—their new temple—a plume of smoke arose as it consumed the lamb. The priests chanted beside the altar, lifting up prayers to Adonai, asking the Almighty to intercede for His people.

Odelia's heart ached. Zillah was right. She was no purer or holier than Sherah. Why did she believe so? Because Shaphan had asked her to help lead this group? Because of her knowledge of the underground caves? The knowledge she'd gained in sneaking away from chores and family and putting herself and her cousins in danger?

As the smoke billowed into the air, she felt a great loss for the innocent life of the lamb. Why should it die for her sins and those of her people? And yet, it was the way of the Lord and His Law—was it not even a sin to question it in this moment?

When the prayers and hymns were finished, Odelia dragged herself off the ground and made her way back to the fire. Though she tried to eat slowly, and at times nausea forced her to, Odelia had never tasted food so wonderful. She chewed a soft piece of bread, savoring it.

"You women are very quiet at this meal." Hashem picked the last of the meat off the bone of a chicken leg with his teeth.

Zillah smiled. "We are too busy enjoying the feast."

Hashem eyed Odelia and then Sherah. "It is more than that, but I know better than to poke at an irritable lion."

Sherah bared her teeth, and Hashem shrugged, continuing with his chicken. "See? Tense."

After they finished eating, they used a small clay pot Zillah had brought to make a bone broth that would sustain them and keep up their strength in the coming days. Zillah pulled out pouches of dried herbs and added them to the pot.

From a few fires away, the cry of a woman rose to meet their ears. Through the tents, Odelia glimpsed a boy about Hashem's age clinging tightly to his forearm, red seeping through his fingers. Zillah grabbed for her bag. "Odelia, come. I may have need of you."

Odelia followed, unsure what help she could offer. When they reached the group, the woman pressed her dirtied tunic to the boy's wound and glanced around with wide, crazed eyes. "We need a doctor."

Zillah knelt by the boy, reaching for a clean linen cloth from her bag. "I do not think there is a doctor among us, but I practice the art of healing. I may be of help. What happened?"

The boy didn't answer. His face grew as pale as goat's milk beneath his dark hair. His imma tried to control her sobs. "They were playing with the swords."

Zillah's eyes widened as she guided the boy to lie on the ground. Eliana propped a blanket beneath him.

"We must keep the arm elevated above the center of the body to stop the bleeding. Odelia, come support his arm while I clean the wound."

Odelia scurried over to kneel by the boy, who was visibly shaking beneath the hot sun. Zillah spoke to him in calming tones, telling him to close his eyes and breathe air into his lungs—that he would heal if he gave his body the air it needed. Odelia grew dizzy at the sight of the boy's lifeblood oozing from the wound and averted her eyes, following Zillah's instructions to breathe deeply until she could bring herself to study her new friend's ministrations.

Zillah ordered water be brought to her and soaked clean linen rags in it. She washed the wound then dressed it with an unguent of olive oil, frankincense, and cumin. Finally, she wrapped it expertly in a makeshift linen bandage. The boy's abba—one of the soldiers—helped move him into a tent away from the harsh sun. Zillah propped blankets under his arm and handed his imma a pouch of herbs. "Brew this for the boy and keep him drinking it throughout the night. I will check on him before dusk."

When they ducked from the tent, the boy was breathing easier, as was his imma.

Odelia stared at Zillah as if seeing her for the first time. "You are extraordinary."

Zillah shook her head. "My *savta* taught me. She is the finest midwife in all of Jerusalem."

Odelia pressed her lips together, wishing she'd had a grandmother of her own. "She…stayed behind?"

Zillah blinked fast, the first sign of emotion Odelia had seen from her. "Yes. She did not believe Adonai would allow the destruction of the city. She insisted her patients needed her."

"I am so sorry, Zillah." They had vowed to be sisters, but how much did Odelia know about this woman? About Sherah? So very little.

Zillah nodded. "The journey we face is not easy." She readjusted her bag over her shoulder. "Neither the physical one nor the emotional one. But Adonai is with us."

Odelia's thoughts drifted back to the city she had called home. "What of those left behind? They do not have the ark. Perhaps the temple is burning even now. Is Adonai with them?"

Zillah swallowed. "Perhaps that is a better question for your scholar."

Odelia bit her lip. "Perhaps."

When they reached their campfire, Zillah checked on the broth simmering over the heat. Inside the tent, Sherah arranged blankets. Odelia had to admit her old friend had managed to make the tent as cozy as was possible in the middle of the desert.

"May I speak with you?" Odelia asked.

Sherah said nothing but continued removing a rock from beneath a blanket she had laid down.

"I wish to apologize for what I said earlier. It was haughty and prideful, and I should not have said it."

Sherah smoothed the blanket, not showing any sign of having heard Odelia.

"I do not know what more to say. But I am sorry. Please forgive me." She stood in stilted silence for another moment, the breeze in the open plain flapping at the thin wall of the tent. She turned to leave.

"Sisters do not always agree." Sherah's words stopped her before she pushed open the hanging flap of goatskin.

"Yes, that is true."

"This does not change our covenant."

Odelia nodded. "No, it does not."

Not exactly a gesture of forgiveness but one of agreement. They would continue onward as sisters as best as they were able. In their weakness, in their searching for belonging in a world that was no longer familiar.

They were sisters. Come what may.

CHAPTER ELEVEN

Three more days of travel brought them into the Valley of Achor. The ragged, dusty land was barren of vegetation and people. Save for four gaunt travelers with their eyes toward the south, they were without company, although Odelia could not shake the notion that at any moment, the Babylonians would come upon them, would pillage the ark and take the stowaways captive.

Rugged gorges filled the land—gone were the olive trees and grasses of Jerusalem. In their place lay only terra-cotta rock, limestone cliffs, desert, and abundant caves. The latter would at least provide a plethora of hiding places for the temple treasures.

Whether their group ultimately settled in this valley or not, it made for an appropriate place for them to rest now. To worship. To renew their sapped strength.

Still, visions of Sodom and Gomorrah haunted Odelia. This was the place, in the stories of Joshua, where Achan was stoned to death for plundering the city of Jericho after Yahweh had instructed otherwise. Because of one man's sin, the Hebrew army had been defeated in their next campaign.

One man's sin.

On their first night in an abandoned village of goatherds west of the Jordan, not far from the Salt Sea, Odelia enjoyed the warmth of the fire alongside Zillah, Sherah, and Hashem. The group had spent the day scouting the caves in the area called Secacah, setting up their tents and fires and provisions, and gathering wild locusts to eat. The priests had set up the Tent of Meeting once again, and they had eaten a dinner of goat meat and bread.

Her stomach fluttered at the sight of Aden approaching their fire. He hadn't sought her out since that first night, no doubt busy with the many duties of the tabernacle. Now, Odelia didn't miss how Hashem perked up at the sight of the man.

"Shalom," Aden said, addressing the three women and the boy at the fire.

"Shalom," they answered.

"How do you fare? I heard the boy Jared's arm is healing well, thanks to your skill, Zillah."

Zillah dipped her head. "I am grateful to be of help, more grateful Adonai saw fit to aid in his healing."

Aden's gaze traveled over Odelia and then moved to Sherah. The woman had seemed to fill out in all the right places with only a few days of sufficient food. Her face shone full and glowing by the light of the fire, and she cast the entirety of her charms on Aden. "You have done an admirable job of leading us here."

One corner of Aden's mouth lifted. "A good map and skilled soldiers work wonders." He turned to Hashem. Sherah seemed to wilt at the shift in attention.

"I think now might be a good time to show me your skill with a sling."

Hashem popped up, quicker than a gazelle on a hunt. "Yes! I saw an oryx not far from here. I can try to scout him out."

Aden seemed to size up the child. "What is your name, boy?"

"Hashem."

"Hashem. I am Aden ben Baruch."

"I do not have an abba or imma, so I am just Hashem. But if I need a formal name, I should like Hashem ben Shaphan."

Odelia swallowed back a lump the size of an almond. This boy may be her final undoing.

Aden's deep eyes twinkled with that familiar depth from the light of the fire. Was he understanding the connection he shared with the boy? One of being an orphan under Shaphan's care? "That does have a nice ring to it."

Hashem grinned and grabbed his sling. He started to lead the way then stopped. "You should come also, Odelia. You have not seen my slingshot skills yet."

Odelia hesitated.

"Yes, come." Aden's eyes held a hint of amusement. She didn't think it possible to ever grow tired of those hazel-specked brown orbs. "I wish to speak to you, actually."

Odelia rose, tucking her mantle more tightly around her. She felt the weight of Sherah's glare on her back as she walked away from their fire with Aden and Hashem.

Aden turned to look at her. "Were you able to visit the Salt Sea today with the other women?"

"Yes, it was wonderful." Though the water was not drinkable, bathing after the long journey refreshed her beyond measure.

"Did you float, Odelia? Did you know the water makes you float?" His eyes twinkled.

She tried to hide her blush. "I did."

"I should like for us to swim together sometime," Hashem said.

Aden smiled and patted the boy's shoulder. "Perhaps you can join the men tomorrow, Hashem."

The boy puffed out his chest. "I would like that." He squinted his eyes at the pack of dry brush ahead, where something rustled in the brambles. "I will return."

Aden and Odelia followed along at a slower pace, both laughing softly at the boy's enthusiasm.

"What do you think of our new home?" Aden asked.

Odelia scanned the barren limestone and sandstone cliffs and caves surrounding them. One wadi to their north and one to their west bordered the rough terrain. The scent of salt and myrrh from the nearby sea tinged the air, though not so much as a single date palm graced the landscape.

"It is dusty."

"It is. But it is undefiled. We can cleanse ourselves in the sea. The Jordan is not far, although it may be dried up with the drought. Some of the soldiers will travel south to Ein Gedi tomorrow. There is an oasis where they can secure water. When they return, they will begin digging the cistern, and we will continue to pray Adonai sends rain."

"Ein Gedi." The name was familiar to Odelia. "Is that not the place King Saul hunted down King David?"

Aden raised an eyebrow. "I must say, for one who does not read, you have quite a memory for Scripture."

A blush climbed Odelia's neck. "It is not so hard to remember when one finds something interesting."

"I suppose not."

"I am afraid my interest also leaves me troubled at times."

"How so?"

Odelia looked off to the horizon, where the sun turned the color of red lentils. "I cannot stop thinking of those left behind in the city."

"Neither can I."

She studied his handsome profile, the way he walked with the stance of a soldier but did not once flaunt either his physical looks or his capable mind. "I try to take comfort in the promise that Adonai is with us. But what of the others?"

Aden watched Hashem squat low to the ground, scouting out the dry brush, sling poised. He stopped a hundred cubits away from the boy, giving him space to continue his hunt. From his position, Hashem turned to look at them, ensuring they watched his every move. Seeming satisfied, he returned his focus to his prey.

Aden softly cleared his throat. "I have immersed myself in Scripture and in Jeremiah's scrolls, and still, I am not sure I have a clear answer for that. All I know is we must grieve."

She squinted at him in the fading light. "You are not uncomfortable admitting you do not have an answer for me?"

"Do you think less of me? For that may very well dull my pride."

She smiled. "Not at all. In fact, quite the opposite. It makes me feel less alone to know even a future priest ponders the mysteries of Yahweh."

"I told you before I am not confident in my imminent position as a priest. It makes me uncomfortable to think I should have answers others do not."

"Yet you know the Scriptures."

He studied Hashem, the setting sun glinting off the wheat specks of his eyes. An invisible pull came upon her. A draw to not only his handsome looks but to his openness. To his heart.

She held her breath, waiting for his next words.

"The priests who did not heed Jeremiah's warnings also knew the Scriptures."

True. "It is a great responsibility."

"Those who claim to know all there is to know of Adonai hide behind their supposed knowledge. They build a god they can understand, one who looks more like them than Adonai. And when Yahweh does speak, they are so anxious to stand firm on the rock of their own imaginings that they do not realize it was hollow and crumbling to begin with."

"Men like my abba." She watched Hashem poise his sling and take aim.

"I did not know your abba as you did."

"You are being kind. You know he had Jeremiah flogged. Certainly, you know he never looked after the poor, paid little attention to the widows, and encouraged King Zedekiah to renege on his ruling to free the slaves."

"And yet you are not like him."

She didn't dare meet his gaze, instead watched Hashem's stance grow rigid as he spotted something in the brush. Then, in a move she could not comprehend, he allowed his whirling sling to tilt slightly west, away from his victim, before letting his sling fly. The animal skittered away.

Hashem stood and shrugged. "I missed."

Odelia narrowed her eyes at the boy. *Hmm.*

"Next time then." Aden smiled. "It was an admirable attempt. You are stealthy."

Hashem's shoulders slumped as he walked toward them. Odelia ruffled his hair. "At least we have already had our dinner. Perhaps you can try again tomorrow morning after the call to the tabernacle."

The threesome walked back toward the fire. Several cubits from their tent, Aden bid them good night, saying he must speak to one of the priests. He thanked Hashem and Odelia for the walk, leaving the pair to meander back to their tent.

"Hashem?"

"Yes?" The boy gazed at a campfire at the mouth of a distant cave where some of the families had taken shelter.

"You could have killed that oryx, I think."

The boy did not answer.

"Why did you not?" She tempered her tone, coaxing him.

"I am a terrible soldier."

She knelt to better look into his eyes. "What do you mean?"

"I could have made the shot. I know my skill. We could have been having oryx to break our fast tomorrow."

"I am not angry. Only curious."

Hashem stared off at the darkening horizon. "I spent the last few days watching that animal to better understand how it thinks, where it feeds. When it came time to end its life, I could not do so. Please do not tell Aden."

She fought the urge to squeeze the boy to her chest. "It will be our secret."

"A most shameful one."

She tapped the spot beneath his chin. "A good soldier suffers and bears the deepest scars of battle, and they are not found on his skin—they are found here." She placed her hand over his small chest. "There is wisdom in hesitating before taking life, Hashem. There is no shame in that."

One side of his mouth lifted. "Only shame if you find yourself hungry tomorrow morning."

Odelia laughed. "Fortunate for you we have enough food for the time being."

At the fire, Zillah mended a hole in her pack, and Sherah attempted to weave a basket from dried reeds she'd found near one of the wadis.

"Well?" Zillah scooted next to Odelia after she sat.

"Well, what?" Odelia tried to keep her lips from twitching.

"What did you speak of? What did he say? He likes you, that is certain."

Odelia's skin grew warm, despite the rapidly cooling night. "He is being friendly."

Zillah raised her eyebrows to convey she didn't believe Odelia then went back to her sewing.

"He did say some of the soldiers are traveling to Ein Gedi tomorrow to seek water. Do you know if Jehoahaz will be among them?"

"I am not certain. We have not spoken much since our arrival. He is busy with organizing."

Sherah sighed and stood, flinging down her unfinished basket. "These reeds are too brittle. I am tired. Shalom." She pushed aside the flap of their small tent and disappeared inside.

"Once the soldiers bring back water, we will all be in better spirits." Zillah pushed a slim bone needle through the material of her bag.

"Yes." But Odelia stared at the tent flap, waving in the desert breeze. She wondered if she and Sherah would ever live in the sisterhood of their verbal covenant. Or if perhaps, Sherah, like her, was beginning to regret their covenant already.

CHAPTER TWELVE

"What if Yahweh is displeased we are tucking Him away in a cave?" Odelia allowed the question to linger in the late afternoon air as she and Aden walked in a wide circuit around their camp, as had become their habit. The wind from the east cooled her skin, bringing with it the deep mineral scent of the sea.

Though he often sought her company, she never ceased to be surprised when he approached. They were both without parents to oversee talks of a betrothal contract, and yet it seemed obvious that, despite her weak tongue, Aden was interested in *her*.

The thought caused Odelia to smile into her goatskin blanket at night. The joy of it took some of the sharp sting from the pain of leaving everything behind.

Now, Aden's mouth twitched, as it tended to do at many of her questions.

"I very much doubt that mere humans can tuck the Creator of All Things away, as if He is not able to burst out if He so chooses," he said.

"You mock me."

After much deliberation between the priests and soldiers, it was decided to move the temple treasures into a nearby cave to give better security to Yahweh's dwelling place. As they watched the priests, adorned in their clean robes, carry the ark to its new hiding place, Odelia felt a surge of loss. She had visited the tabernacle often, worshiping within distance of it. Now His dwelling would again be hidden.

"No, I enjoy teasing you. Forgive me." Aden raked a hand through his hair. His beard had grown longer in the weeks since they'd arrived in the old goatherds' village, making him even more attractive.

They had been here for weeks now, undisturbed. It did indeed seem they'd found a haven.

But the soldiers returning with water did not improve Sherah's disposition. Neither did the building of the stone oven, which ensured them fresh bread, or the rainstorm which had gathered the first of their fresh water in the new cistern and seemed to signal the end of their long draught.

Aden sighed. "I suppose I am not convinced that Yahweh resides in the ark of the covenant. I have been studying Jeremiah's scroll and it says there will come a time when the ark will not be remembered or even missed."

She remembered him saying as much when they first met in the temple with Shaphan and the others. Still, she could scarcely imagine it. "You truly believe there will be a time without the ark?"

Aden nodded, his mouth pressed in a solemn line.

"What else does the scroll say?"

"Perhaps it is time to begin your reading lessons. Then you can read it for yourself. Do you think Hashem would like to join us?"

"Oh yes!"

"We could begin tomorrow, after the morning's sacrifices?"

"That suits me, but are you going to make me wait until I know how to read to tell me what else the scroll says?"

Those eyes, soft as lamb's wool, ignited something in Odelia's chest. This man consumed her senses, her thoughts, her emotions. Though she still mourned greatly for her family and her beloved city, having Aden's walks to look forward to made her new circumstances bearable, almost pleasant.

"That would prove good motivation, would it not?"

"Is not the Word of Yahweh to be delivered expediently? Did Adonai give Jeremiah a message that he buried in a field for years before presenting it to the people?"

Aden released a deep baritone laugh that traveled all the way down to Odelia's toes. "No, that He did not. A loincloth He told him to bury, but not His words. I should know by now not to try to best you, should I not?"

She raised her chin. "I suppose you should."

"Very well then. I have been studying another part of the scroll. A most exciting part."

"And it confirms that Yahweh will not always reside in the ark of the covenant?"

He nodded.

"Will another dwelling place be built for Him? How will we worship?"

"These are answers I do not have, questions I share alongside you."

She groaned.

"I told you I will make an inept priest."

She waved off his words. "Does it say what will happen to the ark? Does it give us any direction in how to proceed or will the treasures be buried in a cave by the Salt Sea for all time?"

He shook his head, his mouth firm. "That is not how I interpreted it, although I am anxious to hear what Eliashib thinks."

"What else does the scroll say? What is the exciting part?"

"You are likely familiar with the earlier writings and prophecies of Jeremiah, of his commission by Yahweh to 'uproot and tear down, to destroy and overthrow.'"

"Yes. My abba was not too keen on his prophecies."

"There is more, though—most of which Jeremiah wrote recently, while in the military garrison. It speaks of the other part of his commission. To build and to plant."

The wings of a butterfly fluttered in her stomach. Had she missed the part where Adonai had told Jeremiah to build and plant? Quite likely. Her abba did not believe Jeremiah a true prophet, and so he did not care to repeat his prophecies. What she knew of them was more gossip and rumors around town and in the temple. Yes, she'd heard the prophet speak a few times, but while her memory was good, she was not gifted. And here was something Aden had possession of—another part of Jeremiah's scroll—the part that spoke of hope.

Her heart picked up a steady beat, knocking against her breastbone. "Tell me." The words were scarcely more than a croak from her lips.

"Are you sure you do not wish to wait and read them yourself?"

"No, I do not wish to wait!" She reached out a hand to slap him playfully as she might Hashem when he teased her, but she caught herself before her fingers touched the fabric of his cloak.

"Very well. I have read the words often, even committed them to memory. I believe they are meant to be a symbol of hope for those of us who are left."

Those who were left.

Aden paused, seeming to acknowledge their shared loss. "Do you remember the clay pot I carried here?"

She nodded, also recalling a different clay pot. The broken one Jeremiah had thrown before her abba and the other priests and leaders. The one accompanied by words that spoke of ruin and destruction, the one that had haunted her dreams for as long as she could remember. "Yes. You mentioned it contained a deed. To land Jeremiah had purchased in Anathoth for seventeen shekels."

His smile lit the dusky night air. "Yes." His expression turned serious, inward, as if he battled something she could not see. "I must admit, when I first heard that my abba had overseen the transaction, that the jailers scoffed as Jeremiah bought the land for such a paltry sum, and more so, of the promise that came with it, I was ashamed. My faith wavered in that moment. Like Jacob, I wrestled with Adonai. He gave me strength to consider this deed as more than a common field purchased for an insulting sum."

Odelia stumbled over his words. Adonai had given Him strength. What a beautiful notion. Could such a thing ever happen to her?

"What promise came with the deed?"

Aden continued. "The promise that houses, fields, and vineyards will again be bought by our people in the land of Judah. The promise that Adonai will not forget us. That there will be a new covenant."

Odelia's mouth grew dry. "I wish to hear more."

Aden's gaze grew more intense, those piercing eyes hooking Odelia's very being, as he began to recite the scroll. "'The days are coming,' declares the Lord, 'when I will make a new covenant with the people of Israel and with the people of Judah...'" He paused, wetting his lips. "'This is the covenant I will make with the people of Israel after that time,' declares the Lord. 'I will put my law in their minds and write it on their hearts. I will be their God, and they will be my people. No longer will they teach their neighbor, or say to one another, "Know the Lord," because they will all know me, from the least of them to the greatest,' declares the Lord. 'For I will forgive their wickedness and will remember their sins no more.'"

Unbidden emotion rose in Odelia's throat, surprising her when it slipped into the air between them. The words rushed through her, warming every corner of her, from the tips of her fingers to the tips of her toes, in a great swell, in an outpouring of unexpected grace. "Please, can you repeat that?" She'd never been thirstier for such beauty, such life-giving water.

When Aden complied, she soaked the words in like curds of milk soak up the liquid when churned.

A new covenant. One Adonai would write on the tablet of hearts. A knowing of Him, a time of being with Him without struggling to know every jot and tittle of the Law. All would know Him. From the least...to the greatest. Yahweh would forgive. He would not remember the sins of the past.

She sucked in a giant, cleansing breath, allowing cool air to sweep in to wash her lungs of the tightness that had plagued her for weeks, months, years even. "How will it be so?"

Aden shook his head. "It is not outlined other than to speak of another king. A king from the line of David who will return us to our land. We do not know how it will play out. It is merely a promise to cling to."

"Merely? Merely!" She scoffed at the word. "It is not *merely* anything. It is the most beautiful thing I have heard. We must tell the others. Do they know? Have the priests read this scroll?"

"The priests have been reading it."

"And what do they make of it?"

"They are trusting Adonai for the provision He promises."

"That is all? Should it not be read to the people? Does it not say, 'from the least to the greatest?' Aden, Hashem, and all the women and children and soldiers should hear this every day until it is made known."

Aden's face colored. "You—you may be correct. Perhaps we have not been faithful."

She reached out a hand, and this time she touched the linen fabric of his tunic. "No. No, you have done the very opposite. In these words, you have given me life. I wish to hear more."

They continued walking, circling the camp at a distance, the words warming her when the chill of night crept in. Aden recited lengthy passages, and Odelia drank them in. Promises of restoration from captivity, of freedom from captors, of peace and security amid discipline, of restoration and honor and belonging, of a gathering of Adonai's people—including the poor and the lame and the pregnant immas, of deliverance and comfort and joy, of a new covenant and most precious of all, of a promise that Adonai would be with them through it all.

When he was done, Odelia asked him to recite the words again, despite her fear he would grow tired of them, and of her. If she could hear them enough, they would soak into her mind and spirit. Perhaps, as Jeremiah's words foretold, Adonai would inscribe them with a stylus on her heart.

When darkness began to overshadow the expansive sky and they made their way back to the fires, Odelia sighed with contentment. "I cannot wait to learn to read."

Aden chuckled. "You will learn quickly. I have no doubt."

She stopped walking, turned to him. "Thank you. Aden, thank you so very much."

"Your zeal for learning and Yahweh's Word reminds me of my imma."

"I am certain her passing was a great loss."

"It was. But her faith is not lost. I told myself I would not think about marriage until I found a woman who mirrors the zeal she possessed for Adonai."

Odelia swallowed. A pleasant dizziness came over her, her knees the consistency of soft sheep's cheese. She should tell him she did not have a dowry—not like Sherah. She had nothing, in fact. A worn bag, a blanket, and a prayer shawl were the entirety of her possessions. She had no family to call her own, and now no home. All she held were the promises Aden had just read to her.

Somehow, in this moment though, it seemed enough.

"Odelia, I have spoken to Eliashib about a possible betrothal contract."

She opened her mouth, but no words came forth.

"You have no abba I may approach, and I did not know how to proceed." He rubbed the back of his neck, staring off to the east, to the faint glimmer of the Salt Sea against the setting sun. "He agreed it a wise match, but before he drew up such a contract, I wished to know your thoughts."

Her vision blurred. Her ears rang. Did she hear correctly? He wished to wed her?

She moved her tongue around, grasping for something to say.

"I realize it is soon after so much loss, and we are unsettled, but there is no one else I would like by my side as we seek Adonai's will for His treasures and His people."

She shook her head. "Me?"

He grinned. "Of course, you."

She blew out a long breath, aching for him and aching for the loss she knew was to come with her words. "I have no silver, Aden. Nothing to give you for the bride-price. My abba did not—"

His abrupt laugh cut off her words.

"What?" She bit her lip, hurt molding her insides like a potter's hand molding clay.

"Odelia, I do not care for earthly means. If it were so, I would have taken my chances staying in Jerusalem and being carted off by the Babylonians, who at least know how to live richly. I am not seeking silver, beloved. I am seeking you."

The words stirred a sweet wind over and through her. "But surely—"

"I have no interest in advancing an estate. I have no interest in anything but carrying out Adonai's will. And as a priest, I will always be provided for. I do not want or need any money from you, Odelia. All I want is your heart."

The backs of her eyelids burned. "Then take it. Aden, it is yours already," she choked out.

He stepped closer, lifting a hand to her headscarf. "You agree? I may have Eliashib sign the contract and bring it before the other priests?"

"Tonight, if it pleases you."

He raised his fingers to her face, caressing the delicate line of her jaw, inching closer.

She swayed nearer, drawn to his scent of cedar and hyssop. His calloused fingers traced along her jaw toward her ear. Her breathing came faster, the moment consuming. His breath played along her lips, and then, in a soft brush, they moved over hers in a kiss that marked her like the impression of hot wax over a missive. She was his.

"I have nothing," she whispered.

"That is not true. We have Adonai, and we have this undertaking. We have a hope for our future."

Her spirit sang. Here, it seemed, was a glimpse of Adonai's promises being fulfilled already. A new beginning, a new family, to go with a new covenant. Could it be true?

Visions of her abba in his priestly robes, entering the temple came to mind. Respected, revered, he never set a toe out of line while out of the house, never hinted at his true character. Some, like Shaphan, knew, but many did not.

Odelia gazed at Aden, swiping aside the doubts tugging at the fringes of her happiness. Aden was nothing like her abba. He would never turn into someone so cruel, no matter how long they were wed. Cruelty was not something that came from all priests, or all men for that matter.

He reached for her hand, dispelling all the doubts from her with a single brush of his lips to her fingers. Her insides quivered like an arrow on a tight bow. "I did not expect you when I left Jerusalem, Odelia. But I am overjoyed I found you."

She blinked away tears. "I feel the same."

"I will speak to Eliashib about the betrothal contract this very night."

It wasn't until she'd bid Aden good night and slipped into her quiet tent that she thought of Hashem's future. The boy had come to rely on her. He may be nine and in many ways older than his years, but she could not leave him an orphan. Would Aden allow him into their new life together, or would he begrudge the boy's presence once they were married?

She fell asleep, the excitement of the night and the lingering question about Hashem swirling within her.

CHAPTER THIRTEEN

The invaders pounced in the dark of night like a leopard on its prey.

Odelia woke to a pounding that rattled the earth, the jarring sound shaking her insides from where she slept in the small tent. Women screamed as if being attacked, children's cries pierced the air, the metal on metal of swords cut to her ears. And then, the worst of it—grown men shrieking as if being tortured.

Odelia's skin crawled as she reached for a rock beneath her blanket, the only means she possessed to protect herself.

"Hashem?" she whispered. Was the boy safe? He hadn't been in the tent when she'd climbed beneath her blankets.

"He is not here." Sherah's voice came to her strained and tight from across the tent. Her voice sounded muffled, as if she was hiding behind the small pile of supplies they'd accrued, or covered her face with a blanket.

"Zillah?" Her calm tone belied the worry creeping into her chest.

"She left last night to tend to an ailing priest."

Standing on wobbly legs, Odelia clutched the rock tightly in her hand.

"Where are you going?" Sherah's unhinged words barely met Odelia's ears.

"I must find Hashem."

"You will draw attention to us. It is best to stay."

"I—I cannot." Would she stand by while more of her people were attacked? While a small boy was terrorized by an unseen enemy that could elicit such horrible screams from grown men?

With quaking fingers, she moved aside the tent flap, the pointed rock clutched tightly in her fist. By the faint light of the moon, she glimpsed foreign soldiers on horseback, swords glinting near the mouth of one of the caves. One of the priests lay on the ground with an arrow in his chest, the wound darkening his tunic.

Her breaths grew fast, her blood pumping to her head where it formed black spots in front of her vision. Who had attacked them so brutally? And why? Unless... Odelia looked to the cave, hidden several hundred cubits apart from their camp. Had they come for the treasures? For the ark?

She gazed at the priest with the arrow in his chest. If Zillah were here, she could help him. And where was Hashem? Her blood turned cold as she looked again at the wounded priest. Was Aden lying somewhere, just like this man?

Before she could think to move a cubit outside the tent, a hard body crashed into her, sending her backward and reeling inside the shelter. She fell on the unforgiving ground, the back of her head slamming into the rocky earth, the stone in her hand falling to her blanket. When she tried to get up, meaty hands pushed her back on her pallet.

She tried to scream, but no sound came from her mouth. The scent of beer and rancid breath met her nostrils as the man dragged her toward the opening of the tent. She kicked, twisting from his grip, but every time she wriggled away, his meaty hands grabbed her again.

Sherah.

Sherah was here, in the tent. She could raise a rock to the soldier's head, stop him from taking her.

"Sherah!" Somewhere, she found her voice. But still, her childhood friend did not come.

And then, when Odelia thought all her strength had fled her and she would indeed be taken from her people, the hands released her. She scurried toward Sherah, twisting to defend herself again if necessary.

But instead of the soldier, her gaze fell on Hashem, his eyes wide as he stood at the opening of the tent above the body of the Babylonian soldier, his sling poised, his mark true.

"Is he dead?" Hashem's voice shook, and she wanted to crawl to him, take him in her arms, and protect him from all of this.

Instead, she scooted away from the soldier's body, creeping toward a trembling Sherah, who rocked back and forth on her knees.

Hashem tried to drag the soldier out of the tent by his feet, but to no avail. Odelia willed strength into her legs to help him, her knees trembling, her eyes trying not to focus on the face of the man who had attacked her. When they finished their task and her attacker lay outside their tent, she returned to Sherah's side, shaking, her knees bunched up to her body, her arms clutching her legs tight to keep herself guarded and hidden away from the shame that covered her.

"I am sorry." Sherah rocked like a madwoman, as if she were the one who had just been assaulted. "I am sorry." She repeated the words over and over again, but Odelia couldn't voice so much as a syllable to assuage her guilt.

Why had she not done something?

When a man's gasp came a moment later and Hashem entered the tent with a sword glistening with blood, he stood straight before them. "He will not harm you again." His voice was no longer the voice of a boy but the voice of someone Odelia didn't recognize.

She wept. As the sounds of terror and battle surrounded them, she wept for her people all over again. For Aden, his safety unknown. For gentle Zillah, always trying to heal, whether it be body or soul. For Hashem, who could not find it in him to kill an oryx the day before but today had killed a man.

As the attack continued, Odelia thought to exit the tent—to grab a rock or a dropped sword and fight for her people. But her limbs would not obey. It must have only been a few moments, but time seemed to expand with her helplessness. Once, the opening of her tent shimmered with movement, but the sound of a sword in flesh stopped anyone from entering. Odelia's teeth chattered, her entire body trembling. All she wanted was to seek refuge in the cave where the ark was hidden.

The ark of the covenant. The place of the mercy seat. The symbol of Adonai's presence.

Aden said Yahweh may not be contained in the ark any longer, that a new covenant was coming.

But what good were the covenants made with a friend like Sherah or a covenant made with a God who allowed such torture and pain and turmoil into the lives of His children? If the ark no longer bound Yahweh, why hadn't He been with her this night?

She'd been so hopeful about Jeremiah's writings. Hopeful about the future. But for the first time since leaving the city, she doubted the prophet. She doubted Aden. She doubted Shaphan.

And she doubted Yahweh.

The guttural moans of mourning spoke of grief beyond measure. Odelia curled in a ball beside Sherah, numb and unable to move, praying nonsensical, silent pleas for Aden, Hashem, and Zillah. For all of them. She recognized a few words the soldiers yelled in Aramaic. Something about the king being spotted north. Then the sound of pounding horses faded into the distance. Quiet blanketed the early morning.

Her entire body felt as if it had been pushed through an olive press. She thrust herself up and stumbled out of the tent, unable to avoid the bloodied sights before her. The site of the tabernacle appeared to be empty. When she caught a glimpse of Aden's familiar cloak several cubits off, she cried out, her breaths hitching fast and squeezing the life from her lungs. No. No, Aden could not be dead. They planned a future together. He was young and wise.

"Aden, no. Please, please, no. Adonai." She may have doubted Yahweh, but here and now, there was nowhere else to turn. Odelia crept toward Aden on her knees, the rough rocks scraping her skin through her thin tunic. Half expecting an enemy soldier to climb out of a tent, she scrambled forward, her eyes blurry, her throat thick with dust.

Aden lay on his back. His tunic had been torn, and a strip of linen was wrapped around his waist in what looked to be a bloody wound near his rib. "Aden," Odelia whispered. "Aden, please wake."

She wanted to reach out and shake him, touch his sandy beard, reach for the callused fingers that had traced so tenderly along her face the night before.

She pressed his arm, squeezed. "Aden." She spoke louder, gave him a hard shake.

His head moved back and forth, and she threw her arms around his neck, sobbing with relief.

His brow wrinkled in obvious pain. "Odelia?" Haze clouded the sound of her name on his lips, but still, she rejoiced over every syllable and intonation.

"I am here. I am going to find Zillah to help you."

He grabbed for her. "Do not leave."

She settled in the dust. "You need help."

"I was…trying to get to you."

She gave up on not touching him, and smoothed the lines of his forehead. "Shh, they are gone and I am well."

"Eliashib…"

"I—I do not know." She didn't want to tell him that, from the looks of the carnage around her, likely none of the priests survived.

He tried to sit up but winced, curling around himself.

"Do not move." She helped him lie back down, wishing she had Zillah's skill.

"Did they hurt you?" His words came out in grunting fits and starts.

"I am fine. Aden, I must get Zillah and water and medicine. The sun will bake us before long. We need to shelter you. I will be back, I promise."

He groaned, and she took her leave. Picking up the hem of her tunic, she ran farther into camp. The dead lay around her, women cried over their husbands, children over their abbas.

She spotted Eliana carefully washing the body of her husband, ashes strewn upon her head and face. Odelia looked away.

"Odelia!"

She turned and Hashem came flying at her, his tunic, hair, and face matted with dried blood. He flung his arms around her waist and she clung to him, their shared sobs mounting into a chorus of mourning.

After a moment, she pulled back, studying him. "Are you hurt?"

He swiped at his nose with the sleeve of his threadbare tunic. "Those poxy Babylonians were too slow to catch me. I only wish I had been able to kill more of them."

She closed her eyes. Her Hashem. Her sweet, smiling Hashem.

"Do you know where Zillah is? Aden is hurt."

He nodded, pointing her to a tent close to the spot where the tabernacle had stood.

Hashem stayed with Aden while Odelia stumbled toward the tent, stopping short at the sight of her friend lying on a mat, her face pasty and wan. Kneeling by her side, Jehoahaz held her hand. Dried blood covered him—from his dark hair to his leather boots.

Odelia fell to Zillah's side, reaching for her hand. "She is hurt?"

Jehoahaz nodded, his gaze empty. "I should have never brought her here. They..." His words broke off, but the blood still seeping through the fabric at Zillah's chest told Odelia all she needed to know.

CHAPTER FOURTEEN

Odelia's bottom lip trembled. How did she have any tears left to spare? But they came in a fresh torrent. First sadness and then doubt. Zillah couldn't die. Her only true friend, the only one who knew how to heal. What would she do without her? What would they all do?

Odelia reached for the fabric of Zillah's tunic. "Did you bind her tight? She had a mixture to heal wounds—did you apply them?"

"We did all we could. She was still conscious and told me what to do." Then the big soldier broke down and wept.

Odelia looked from Zillah then back to Jehoahaz. Uncomprehending and disbelieving.

Adonai, You told Moses You were a gracious God! This is not grace. We saved the ark only to be caught in the wilderness again, to be left without protection, to have everything taken from us!

Her gaze fell on Zillah's bag. "May I?" she asked Jehoahaz. "Aden is in need."

An imperceptible nod. Odelia took it then leaned and gave her friend's pale forehead a gentle kiss. She placed her hand on her uncovered head. "May Adonai give you peace, my sister."

When her tears began to fall in earnest, she left. She did not stop, despite the many mourners she passed, until she reached Aden.

"Odelia? Odelia!"

She startled, focusing on Hashem at her side, eyes wide. Had he been calling to her? She hadn't even noticed.

Those brown eyes searched her own, asking a myriad of silent questions for which she did not have answers. "What can I do?" he asked.

"Can you find a skin of water? I think there is one in our tent." Briefly, she thought of Sherah, wondering if the woman still hid in the corner of their tent. Well enough. What help could she possibly give?

"Wait."

Hashem turned.

"Tell Sherah that Zillah..." She couldn't finish the words, but the boy understood. He nodded, running off.

Focusing on Aden, she breathed a sigh of relief that his chest rose and fell, that his gaze was alert. She knelt beside him, Zillah's bag in hand.

"She was unable to come?" he asked.

Odelia pressed her lips together and shook her head. Aden's eyes searched the sky, as if he too questioned why Adonai had not protected the very ones who had tried to safeguard the symbol of His presence.

The rising sun beat down on them, dust swirled around them. "We must move you into a tent."

He nodded, trying to push himself up. But just as he managed to sit, his eyes rolled back in his head, and he swayed. Odelia caught him before his head hit the ground.

A moment later, Hashem returned with the water. The boy helped her lift the skin and dribble the water past Aden's lips before they took drinks of their own.

Odelia sat on her haunches, looking for a man who might be able to help her carry Aden. But all around her mourning women and children wept, ashes clinging to their skin, hair, and clothes as they tended to the bodies of their dead. "We must move him." She pointed to the closest tent. "There. Do you think you can help me?" Best move him now, while he was passed out, for surely the pain of being moved would be unbearable.

Hashem nodded. Odelia grabbed Aden's upper body, careful to support his head, while Hashem lifted his legs.

Somehow, they reached the tent, vacant but smelling of last night's dinner. Sweat poured off Odelia's head, her arm and back muscles strained. She led them to a mat, hoping the person who owned it—if still alive—would not be bothered by them commandeering it in such a manner.

Hashem stared at Aden, who was still unconscious. "Now what?"

Odelia swallowed. "I must clean his wound."

"You know how to do that?"

"I watched Zillah once. Leaving it to fester will not do." She tried to remember all Zillah had done for the boy's arm, but the memories clung like a haze in her mind. Was the procedure for a greater wound the same as that of a minor one?

She searched through Zillah's bag, pulling out a roll of linen fabric and several small clay jars alongside a knife and some reeds. Odelia lay aside the one labeled cumin and began to sort through the pouches of herbs. Poppy seeds for pain. Aloe for wounds. Mint oil and hyssop. Zillah had told her she had made a tea of yarrow, echinacea, poppy seed, and lemon balm to fight infection for the boy Jared. From the looks of it, some still remained in her bag.

Odelia raised it to her nose and smelled the unmistakable tangy hint of lemon mingling with the licorice-like scent of the yarrow. She added the herbs to an empty flask, creating a tincture she hoped might save Aden's life and bring him relief.

Aden had spoken of Yahweh giving strength. Could He do so for her now? Then again, why did she continue to ask and seek Him when He had so obviously abandoned them the night before?

She didn't understand. She didn't understand the evil that had come upon them, the pain of her people, of Zillah and Aden, of this group who had been trying to follow Adonai. She didn't understand why that soldier had tried to drag her away with such force.

But in the end, she had nothing else on which to cling. Only Adonai's promises remained.

I will be their God, and they will be My people.

Perhaps the culmination of this promise was yet to be seen, but as Odelia gestured for Hashem to place the skin of water by her side, she continued to pray, hoping she would live long enough to one day see such a promise fulfilled.

She arranged the blankets, and then Hashem helped her gently remove the makeshift bandage Aden had fashioned, along with his tunic. Blood marred his broad, muscled chest and Odelia breathed deeply through her nose. If she fainted along with Aden, who would tend to him? Poor Hashem had borne enough. She could not leave the boy alone.

She breathed in lungfuls of air, the tangy scent of blood causing black spots to dance before her eyes. She turned away to wash her hands and then dipped a linen cloth into the water Hashem had brought. She tried to remove herself from the task, allowing her hands to work while her mind settled into a peculiar, yet comforting, numbness. She cleaned the wound, relieved to see that although it was large, it was not as deep as the blood had made her think.

When she'd cleaned the area as well as she could, she spread Zillah's cumin and frankincense tincture on it along with some precious honey. With Hashem's help, she wound fresh linen tightly around Aden's waist before washing her hands and brewing the tea, dribbling it into his mouth throughout the morning.

Hashem curled at her feet and slept. She studied the boy, his smooth face young and peaceful. He had killed a man. How did that affect one so young? Yes, there was honor in fighting for his people, in trying to protect the ark, but would such circumstances stain the man he'd become? And what of their people? So many had rejected Hashem for his birth heritage, and last night, he had given them everything. Would the boy grow bitter over all they'd taken from him? Would he have been better off left at the city wall that day?

A tear slid down Odelia's cheek, shame rising at the thought. Saving life was always preferable to the ruination of it. Hashem had learned the love of Adonai through Shaphan, through her. She could only pray that last night's horrors hadn't obliterated that love. For him and for her.

The tent flap peeled back, and Sherah appeared, dark circles beneath her eyes. Her gaze moved over Odelia then Hashem, before settling on Aden. "He is wounded?"

"Yes." The cold steel point of a sword was warmer than Odelia's voice.

"Will he live?"

"I pray it is so."

Sherah's bottom lip trembled. "Zillah... She is gone."

Odelia closed her eyes, wanting to block her pain from this woman. This woman who had only added to it.

"Odelia—" Sherah started.

But Odelia shook her head. "Please leave me."

Her childhood friend stood in the opening of the tent for another moment before disappearing.

Hashem stirred, and Odelia sensed him wakening, trying to process all the terrors sleep had persuaded him to forget. He lay still for a long time, his breathing quick and shortened instead of the longer breaths she'd heard while he slept.

"She did not help you." He did not move from where he lay, simply stared at the pointed ceiling of the black goat-hair tent.

"She did not. Perhaps she could not."

"I hate her."

Odelia bit her lip, trying to dig for words to admonish or encourage the boy. She thought of what King Solomon had spoken in the Proverbs scrolls, about giving bread to your enemy when he is hungry, and water to him when he is thirsty, but she couldn't pull the words up into her throat. How could she when her heart mirrored Hashem's? That his words stemmed from loyalty to her caused affection to bloom. And yet hating Sherah would do none of them any good.

"I wish the events of last night had not occurred. I wish you had not been compelled to do what you did. But I am glad you stopped him."

Hashem glared beyond her, at the peak of the tent. "He deserved to die. They all did. I do not regret it." And yet the quiver in his words told her how the killing and fighting had affected him.

She reached for his small shoulder. "I wish I had words of wisdom for you right now, but I am afraid I am bereft."

He curled his head in her lap and she rubbed his back. "I miss Shaphan," he mumbled into the folds of her tunic.

"I do too."

"What do you think he would say to us right now?"

Odelia sighed. "I wish I knew. Perhaps that we should look to Adonai in our pain. Perhaps that there was no way for us to avoid Jeremiah's prophecies, even by leaving the city. Maybe he would tell us to rejoice that we are spared, that we will continue to protect the ark of His presence. I pray he would tell us of the new covenant Yahweh promised."

The words sounded reasonable, even to her own ears. She must only make her heart believe them.

Hashem raised his head off her lap. "What new covenant?"

Had it only been last night that she rejoiced over the words Aden shared with her? Now the entire evening with Aden appeared dulled and tarnished, like an impossible dream. She didn't exactly believe they were untrue—simply that the promise of a new covenant did not apply to her. That joy did not apply to her. It was for her people in the future. Certainly not this ragtag remnant who had tried to do a worthy thing by saving the ark.

Unbidden, tears coursed down her cheeks until her weeping became sobbing and then inarticulate groanings. Deep grief that soaked her being, wrenching wet, choking sobs from her body.

Hashem sat up. "What is it, Odelia? Please do not cry."

She swiped at her face and stood. "I will be back. Fetch me if he wakes." She scurried to her tent, grateful to be alone. She gathered ashes from the firepit and poured them on her head, rubbed the ashes into her skin. She hid herself away in the tent, kicking aside her blanket, and lay uncovered, sobbing on the dirt floor.

CHAPTER FIFTEEN

Odelia went about preparing the bodies for burial and tending the wounded with a heart growing numb to the pain around her, a heart so consumed by its own haunting horrors that it threatened to shrivel like a dried insect.

Of the priests, only two—Aden and Eliashib—had survived. And Eliashib barely at that. The older priest's arm had been cut off, and he suffered a fever. Odelia did all she could think to stanch the blood, to clean the wound, to fight infection. Eliashib's wife Ana was unharmed, but their twelve-year-old son had given his life trying to protect his imma. The tragic news of his son's death did not aid Eliashib in his recovery.

With heavy hearts, they conducted the burials over the next three days. Jehoahaz scouted out a nearby cave that would serve as the burial spot for the seven priests, the three soldiers, Zillah, and Eliashib's son Benjamin.

The preparation and mourning gave Odelia a small sense of purpose amid her grief. She wrapped the bodies in wool with sweet-smelling herbs, the dust and salt from the land mixing with her tears.

Would her limbs ever relax? Her stomach unclench, the muscles in her back loosen? Would she forever anticipate another attack?

Jehoahaz informed them that the Babylonians had been chasing after King Zedekiah and his contingent but had fled the group when word came that the king had been spotted north in the Jordan Valley. Had the king escaped? Did anyone escape from the fierce brutality of such men? And why hadn't the soldiers taken their small group captive? Jehoahaz speculated that they'd been in a hurry and fled quickly to continue their chase. He was confident they did not realize the ark and the temple treasures had been right beneath their noses.

But that did not mean they wouldn't be back.

By the third day, Aden was able to walk gingerly to the funeral biers at the burial site and mourn along with them. Other than checking his bandages once a day, Odelia avoided him. What was there to say? That she no longer felt like the same woman she'd been only three days before? That the event pulled doubts about Adonai, Jeremiah's message, and everything Aden believed to the forefront of her thoughts? That it secured in her the terrors most certainly done to those they left in Jerusalem?

On the fourth night after the attack, she made her way to Aden's tent, Zillah's bag propped over her shoulder. She passed clusters of women and children preparing bread for the evening meal. The yeasty scent tugged at a deep thread of homesickness, threatening to unravel her. The absence of the men who had died cast a heavy cloud over the camp. How would they survive without them? Without the priests to lead them? With only four soldiers left to guide and protect them? She greeted most of the women by name, and they returned their shaloms, but a hollowness resided in their eyes. The same hollowness Odelia suspected they glimpsed in her own gaze.

When she arrived at Aden's tent, she peered beyond the flaps, which had been tied back, and stopped short at the sight of Sherah beside Aden's pallet. The smiles on both their faces disappeared when they spotted her.

Odelia gritted her teeth but managed to stand her ground. What business did the woman have in Aden's tent? Had she so much as lifted a dainty finger to help with the food or children that day?

Sherah stood. "I had best begin preparing for Shabbat." Odelia glared after the woman's retreating footsteps.

"Shalom, Sherah," Aden called out.

Odelia knelt beside Aden.

"Shalom, Odelia."

"Shalom."

He arranged the blankets and lifted his tunic in what was becoming a familiar routine between them.

"I see you are feeling better." She unwound the bandage.

"Sherah was telling me a story of her childhood. Of spilling an ephah of barley flour in her kitchen and her abba teaching her the alphabet by drawing in the mess."

Odelia kept her gaze on her ministrations. "Sherah was fortunate to have loving parents."

She studied the wound. Though the gash was not pleasing to the eye, neither did it bear angry red marks signaling infection. "It is healing."

He glanced at the lesion. "I have a good healer."

Odelia swallowed. "Zillah would have been better." She couldn't help reminding him of all they'd lost, all that night had cost them. How could he sit in the tent and laugh with Sherah while so many around them suffered?

She applied the last of the cumin oil. She'd make more after dinner. Her thoughts quieted when Aden reached for her hand. She stilled beneath his touch, her gaze moving to his.

The deep eyes she'd come to love searched her own, moving back and forth as if studying a precious jewel. "Thank you, Odelia. You likely saved my life."

She pressed her lips together and slid from his touch, searching for a fresh bandage in Zillah's bag—her bag. "Surely you know I would not leave you to die."

His throat bobbed. "I was trying to get to you." His voice strained, caught around a lump it seemed. "I fought with my sword. If I had given equal attention to weapon training as I did to my scrolls, perhaps I would have made it in time."

"It is not for you to feel guilt over."

He grew serious. "Sherah said a soldier was in your tent…"

Odelia's face flamed as she concentrated on winding the bandage around Aden's muscled torso. "Yes."

"Odelia."

She could not look at him. If she met those eyes, she would break down in a pathetic lump of grief and regret. She focused on his bandage, securing it in the folds she'd wound. When she was finished, he readjusted his tunic.

"You are healing well." She kept her voice distant, impersonal.

"Odelia."

"If you feel well enough to walk, I think some daily exercise will do you good."

"Odelia."

She met his gaze, even while knowing she would regret the action.

"Did he harm you?"

She swallowed, gathering her supplies. "Who?"

"The soldier." His patient kindness wore on her.

"Do you not think Sherah would have told you if he had?"

The look on Aden's face turned to flint. "I am not asking Sherah. I am asking you."

She pulled the flap over Zillah's bag and stood. "I am unharmed."

And she was, wasn't she? The wounds she bore were etched upon her heart, not her flesh.

He released a long exhale. "I am glad. I have not had a chance to tell you—Eliashib signed the betrothal contract that very night."

She inhaled a short take of air. She was betrothed then. In the eyes of the Law and of Adonai, she was married. All that was left to be added was a ceremony that would usher her into her husband's home, where they would sleep as one.

She stared outside the tent, to where a girl of about seven walked by. Rachel, Odelia thought her name was. A daughter of one of the priests. A now fatherless girl who would never forget the terrors of the night that had stolen her abba from her. A girl who would enter womanhood without the protection of an abba.

A lump rose in Odelia's throat. "Much has changed since then." *She* had changed. For yes, she was fortunate Hashem had saved her from the soldier, but what of the constant fear that now plagued her? What of the faith Aden had praised her for that seemed to have vanished with the notion of safety? Shame bubbled up within her at the thought. Was she no better than her father, looking to gods of prestige and security instead of the One True God?

With obvious effort, Aden stood, his head nearly bumping the top of the goatskin tent. "My intentions have not." He came closer, the heat of his body inches from her own. He raised a hand and caressed her face much as he did the night of the attack.

She pulled away. "I am sorry, Aden. I—I cannot." She ducked out of the tent, walking with quick steps toward her own tent, each step taking her farther from the object of her pain, farther from all the impossible hopes she'd once held for herself, and for her people.

The following weeks dragged out as hunger again overtook their small community. Aden did not speak again of the betrothal contract. Law dictated they wait at least a month before occupying the same living space.

Though rumors of the group moving south flitted through their camp, they remained at Secacah. It wasn't difficult to know why, for how could they carry the ark with only two priests, and one of them without an arm?

Odelia did not sleep well at night, both fear and hunger pains making her body ache. While Hashem had killed an oryx with his sling, the meat and the last of their grain did not fill them for long.

Jehoahaz sent Omri with a detachment of boys that included Hashem to Ein Gedi to gather supplies and forage what they could. When they returned two days later, Odelia noted Hashem's confident carriage, the couple of inches it seemed he'd grown since they left Jerusalem…the new hardness that molded him. She already missed the boy she'd once known, but they were all changing under their circumstances, weren't they? She only prayed those changes honored those who had died at the hands of their enemy.

The day they returned, Aden approached Odelia as she organized the last of the herbs in Zillah's bag.

"Shalom," he called.

"Shalom."

He looked well. His color healthy, his posture straight. How close had she been to adding him to the list of things that had been lost to her past?

"May we walk?"

She bit her lip. The last time they walked together was that beautiful, fateful, horrible night of the attack.

"I must finish this." She avoided his gaze.

"I will wait."

She finished her task with deliberate slowness, grieving the openness she had once shared with him. A deep loneliness wound around her, ribbons of sadness rippling through her.

Once she finished arranging the herbs, she tucked the bag into the corner of her tent and walked alongside him in the direction of the Salt Sea. To their left lay the hill they'd dubbed Kohlit, beneath which the temple treasures, including the ark, had been hidden.

Was Adonai still with them, seated upon the mercy seat? Or had He fled when they dared take His treasures out of the Holy City?

"Omri and the boys brought back a good supply of food," Aden said.

"They did well."

"You are doing a fine job as a healer." Aden shielded his eyes from the sun to better see the rocky outcropping of caves and limestone stretching toward the sea.

The last week had sealed her position as the healer in their community, no matter that her experience paled in comparison to Zillah's. "I am learning as I go. It is not nearly enough."

"We are grateful for you." They walked in silence for several more moments before he spoke again. "I have spoken with Eliashib, Jehoahaz, and the other soldiers."

All the men that remained.

"I must step into the role for which I have been training."

The priesthood. "Of course. It is not reasonable for one priest alone to care for Adonai's dwelling place." She stopped walking. "How do you feel about this?"

"Unprepared. It is a great responsibility to bring the people's sins before Yahweh, to seek to atone for them with the sacrifices." He paused. "Eliashib refuses to take on the mantle of the high priest."

Of course. The Law forbade anyone with a physical defect to approach the curtain or the altar. To approach the ark.

Odelia blinked away tears. "You will make a worthy high priest, Aden, for your heart is for our people, and you are not blind to your own pride."

A soft smile curved his mouth, pulling a sweetness from her insides she'd thought long dead. "I have missed you, Odelia."

"And I, you." It was the truth, even if she should not speak it.

He dragged in a deep breath. "Eliashib does not wish us to put off our union any longer with my anointing ceremony upon us. The thirty days have passed since our contract was arranged."

Her muscles seized, her feet itching to run away from what lay ahead. If she could refuse him without explanation, it would be so much easier. But she was bound to him under the Law now. She *wanted* to be bound to him.

If only...

She shook her head.

"Odelia, what is it? I did not force this upon you in my haste... Did I?"

Unshed tears pricked the back of her lids. "You are a good man, Aden ben Baruch."

"What is it then, beloved?"

"Do not call me that, for it is an endearment I do not deserve."

"You are my *wife*, Odelia. You are my beloved."

"I do not deserve to be your wife." The wife of the high priest. She thought of her imma, offering sacrifices to the queen of heaven while her abba served at the temple. Was she any better, taking on the role of the high priest's wife while clinging to fear instead of faith?

But how could she mold herself into the version of herself Aden expected? The version Adonai expected? How could she make her faith strong again?

Aden placed his hands on her shoulders. "How do you not deserve to be my wife when I am the one who feels so undeserving?"

She bit her lip. The passing of time would not make the telling of the truth any easier. "I—I was...the night we were attacked...the soldier in my tent..." She could not look at him. Instead, she glanced at the sunlight shining off his shoulders.

His jaw hardened. "Did he hurt you?"

She shook her head. "No, not like that. He tried to drag me from the tent. But Aden, I do feel as if I lost something that night." She swallowed, willing the words forth. "My trust in Adonai," she whispered.

His mouth fell open, his hands sliding down her arms. Falling, falling, until they were no longer touching her mantle.

"I am sorry, Aden. Shaphan chose me to help our people on this journey, and I fear I have brought shame on Adonai's people instead."

"We all have times of doubt."

She swallowed. "I am not the woman I was the night we spoke. How can I be the wife of the high priest?"

Aden grew silent for a long while before finally speaking. "'How long, Lord? Will You forget me forever? How long will You hide Your face from me?'"

She stopped. It sounded familiar. Surely the words were not from one of the prophets?

Aden continued. "'How long must I wrestle with my thoughts and day after day have sorrow in my heart?'"

Tears pricked Odelia's eyes. *This* was how she felt. Was Aden reading her heart?

He continued, finishing with a proclamation to trust in Adonai's unfailing love. To trust, despite the doubts.

"It is a psalm of King David."

She pressed her lips together. Did the great king truly once feel the way she did?

"Thank you," she whispered. "I will treasure it." She glanced back at the camp. "I should check what Hashem would like for dinner. He is most certainly famished from his journey."

"We will speak soon, yes?"

Odelia nodded. He stepped forward as if to touch her, but before he could, she turned toward the camp and walked away.

CHAPTER SIXTEEN

That night, after a simple meal of bread and cheese, they gathered by the light of the fires to listen to Aden read the scroll of Jeremiah. Odelia sat on her mat away from the other women.

"May I sit with you?"

Odelia looked up to see Eliana. The older woman's lined face bore the familiar marks of grief, and yet something else cloaked her features—something Odelia longed to have for herself. Determination? Faith, perhaps? A faith Odelia once thought she'd shared with this woman.

No longer.

"Of course."

Eliana arranged her mat beside Odelia's and settled herself. "You must miss Zillah."

Oh, how she missed her friend. The cave and their fires held a lonely quality without her kind, uplifting words. And while Sherah had made meager attempts at conversation, Odelia had attempted none in return. Even Hashem had been scarce of late, likely sensing the pain the two women stirred up with the stink of their fetid silence. Instead, he gathered with his new companions—those with whom he trekked across the desert on the way to Ein Gedi.

"I do. But I am certain it cannot compare to how you ache for your husband. How are you faring, Eliana?"

Odelia gazed at the woman she'd come to admire for her quiet service to the others in their group. Instead of spending her time avoiding Sherah, Odelia could have better spent her time ministering to Eliana and the other widows who lost their husbands in the attack.

She was not the only one hurting. She'd set herself off from the others, set herself apart from Adonai, instead of drawing closer to her God and those around her. They were all that remained.

"I mourn Oren greatly. Perhaps, if we had had children…"

"I am so sorry."

"He could have divorced me long ago for being unable to give him children, give him sons. But he never entertained the idea."

"He must have been a good man."

"He was."

They sat quietly as they watched Aden open the scroll atop a large boulder. Two soldiers held flaming torches on either side of him to give light while Eliashib sat beside him. The older priest was recovering, his wound remarkably bearing no marks of infection.

"We have obeyed Adonai in carrying out this mission. Why then must He make us suffer?" Odelia whispered the words, Aden's distraught face from that afternoon playing in her imagination.

Eliana draped an arm around her and pulled her close. The gesture felt at once both maternal and sisterly. "I am uncertain I have an answer to that one. But Oren used to read the psalms of King David to me. Our king often spoke of the Lord being with him in the midst of his pain."

Odelia bit her lip, unable to bring herself to admit that Aden had recited one such psalm to her earlier in the day.

"'I have come into the deep waters; the floods engulf me. I am worn out calling for help; my throat is parched....'"

Odelia blinked at the recited words, soaking them in, feeling their truth mirroring her own heart. She listened to the rest of the recited psalm, her heart fluttering at the promise at the end.

"'Let heaven and earth praise him, the seas and all that move in them, for God will save Zion and rebuild the cities of Judah. Then people will settle there and possess it; the children of his servants will inherit it, and those who love his name will dwell there.'"

Odelia breathed in the air, slightly smoky from the campfires. Was this the way of faith? To pour one's heart out to Adonai, to wrestle with Him over one's doubts but then to return to His truth? His faithfulness?

She wished she knew.

"Thank you, Eliana."

She squeezed Odelia's arm. "We need one another."

Eliana was right. Odelia had withdrawn into her own grief, pushed aside the other women, pushed aside Aden. It was not the way of their people.

"He is beginning." Eliana gestured toward Aden, who began reading the first words from the scroll of Jeremiah.

Though Aden had recited Jeremiah's words to Odelia the night of the attack, she had only heard summaries of the prophet's writings from others, and once or twice, from the man himself. To hear it all as written in the hand of Aden's abba was sobering, to say the least.

For years, Jeremiah had warned of the consequences of placing their faith in the temple instead of Yahweh. He'd warned of the destruction of her beloved city.

"Will you steal and murder, commit adultery and perjury, burn incense to Baal and follow other gods you have not known, and then come and stand before me in this house, which bears my Name, and say, 'We are safe'—safe to do all these detestable things? Has this house, which bears my Name, become a den of robbers to you?"

Odelia remembered the horrors of the children sacrificed at Ben Hinnom, of the calling of Yahweh that His people turn their hearts to Him. Of Adonai's longing to see His children embrace Him and His *hesed*—the faithful, loving commitment of God to His covenant promise.

"Return, faithless Israel. I will frown on you no longer, for I am faithful. I will not be angry forever."

All of it was foretold to them through Jeremiah's own tears as he wept and pleaded for his people. Odelia sobbed anew when Aden read of her own abba, of the prophecy that haunted her dreams. The disgraceful legacy of her family, how Jeremiah had dubbed her abba's new name to be "Terror on Every Side." How he would see his friends fall by the sword of the Babylonians with his own eyes. How he would be taken into exile—he and his family—to Babylon and there die and be buried among the other priests who had prophesied lies.

She knelt with her head touching the mat, weeping over the final destruction of her abba, over the disgrace of the blood from which she came, over the words of Yahweh's condemnation rolling over her like a chariot wheel does a bruised reed.

This must be why she'd been punished. For surely the name "Terror on Every Side" was to follow her as well. She had not been taken into Babylon. Perhaps this was her punishment—to be broken in faith forevermore.

She thought of Sherah, whom she had judged so severely. What right did she have to cast stones when Jeremiah himself had bestowed such a name upon her abba? When she had sat alongside Sherah listening to the screams outside their tent but doing nothing to help?

Eliana rubbed her shoulder, but the gesture proved little comfort. If Adonai had turned his back on her, what hope did she have?

Aden kept reading. And slowly, the tone of the scrolls changed, snatches of promises catching her in surprise. His voice became like a warm blanket over their group as he spoke not of condemnation, but of assurance, of an undeniable, mounting hope.

Through Jeremiah, Yahweh declared a new day was upon them. He promised to plant and build up. He said He would not hold the people accountable for the sins of their parents.

Hope bloomed in Odelia's chest. She drew a cleansing breath, clinging to that last declaration.

Aden went on to read of Jeremiah's land purchase. A promise of peace and the raising up of a righteous shoot, a branch from David's line who would do what is just, who would save Israel and Judah, and "be called: The Lord our Righteous Savior."

A Savior. Oh, that He might come soon to save them all!

And then, Aden read of the glorious promise of the new covenant. A covenant written on the tablets of hearts. Of blessings in a barren land, of tears of joy overflowing.

Adonai, come to us quickly.

When he stopped reading, it seemed all held their breaths. Odelia felt like a wet rag wrung out to dry. Eliashib prayed over them, and then a boy in the front raised his hand.

"Yes, Hashem?" Aden said.

Odelia perked up.

"When will these things come to pass? When will we be given this new covenant of joy?"

Oh my. Leave it to the young boy to voice so guilelessly what they all so wanted to know.

Eliashib shifted on his mat. "It may not be in our lifetimes. Jeremiah said there will be seventy years of captivity."

Hashem raised his again. "Adonai said the bad figs exiled to Babylon He would turn into good figs—that His future would lie with the exiles. If that is so, should we not want to be among those exiled to Babylon?"

The small gathering grew hushed. A couple of the other boys snickered, but Odelia's head swirled. The boy's question was a good one. And while she only surmised the meaning behind Jeremiah's fig representation, Hashem had seemed to grab onto it without a struggle.

A smile tugged at Eliashib's mouth. "I see we have a bright young scholar in our midst. That is a very good question, Hashem. One I do not have the answer to but one we should think and pray on together."

After a few more comments, the women and children returned to their own fires and caves to settle in for the night. Odelia found Sherah by their fire, struggling to thread a needle. Her childhood friend had taken her time in the menstruation tent the last three days, and it had been a relief not to bear their awkward exchanges. Now though, Odelia bit her lip and sighed.

If the reading of Jeremiah's scroll revealed anything to her, it was the imperfection of her own actions. She was no better than her abba, holding others to impossibly high standards she couldn't keep herself. The time for reconciliation was now.

If only it wasn't so hard to forgive this woman who had stood by and done nothing to help her, the sister with whom she had made a covenant.

CHAPTER SEVENTEEN

"Shalom, Sherah." Odelia crept closer to the dwindling flames of the fire. The hot days gave way to chilly nights, making lungs constrict and bodies tremble. She looked forward to the day when they could shear the few sheep they had and weave warmer blankets for themselves.

Sherah looked up from her sewing, her gaze weary. "Shalom."

How to begin? When Aden read the scroll, Odelia had felt certain of what must be done, had felt the poverty of her own spirit. But now, sitting beside this woman who had been nothing but a burden, who had not helped her in her time of need, and who, in Odelia's irrational thoughts, seemed to be the reason her faith had weakened...what words did she have?

This was too hard. Too difficult a thing for the daughter of a corrupt priest to do.

But then she remembered the foretelling of hope. Of Yahweh's new covenant. If He were to write His character and covenant on the tablet of her heart, how might that change her? How might she handle this moment with Sherah?

She opened her mouth, and what came out was honesty. "I have been angry with you."

The sliver of Sherah's bone needle stilled, but a slight tremor began in her hands.

Odelia shifted where she sat, tucking her mantle more firmly around her legs to keep the warmth in. "I could not understand why you stood by and did nothing when that soldier attacked me."

Sherah did not answer. Odelia bit her lip, questioning the wisdom of what she started. "I realize we have not always been close. But I cannot understand why you did not hurl a skin of water or a rock at his head. You could have stopped him. Stopped Hashem from…"

Still, no answer. Odelia's jaw tightened. She tried her best not to relive those moments, and now, to make amends with Sherah, they haunted her yet again. Why had this woman with whom she'd made a covenant worthy of sisters allowed her such pain?

Slowly, it came to her. "You begrudged my time with Aden," she whispered. "You knew he would not want me if I was defiled. He could not be with me if the soldier took me away."

A choking sound came from Sherah, and she dropped the needle in her lap. She pressed her lips together and shook her head, her pretty eyes brimming with tears that shone by the light of the fire. "Odelia, please. I cannot bear you to think so ill of me."

"Then why? I am trying to forgive you, Sherah, to not hold this bitter root in myself. But it is very difficult."

A wet gulping noise sounded in the back of Sherah's throat. "It is true that I am drawn to Aden and even that I begrudge the attention he pays you."

There. She'd heard all she needed to hear. But now what? Did she come here for a reasonable explanation or to forgive and be gracious, as she begged Adonai to do for her?

"We made a covenant, Sherah. A covenant of loyalty. But it is apparent your promises are no better than those of our people to Yahweh."

A fat tear slid down Sherah's smooth face, and she swiped it away. Odelia straightened, refusing to be moved by the show of emotion.

Sherah stuck a finger through the hole at her hem she'd been sewing, tracing the ragged fabric. "As I said, I did begrudge you… but I am not so horrid that I would be glad to see you taken captive by the Babylonians."

"Then why did you do nothing to stop him?" Her voice came out strident. The women and children in the distance gave Odelia a strange look. Her body trembled. Why had she thought coming to Sherah would honor Adonai, would heal her shattered faith?

"I tried."

The two words caused Odelia to study her childhood friend's serious face. "You seem to forget I was there. You did no such thing."

"Please believe me, Odelia. I tried. I have never been the victim of an evil spirit, but one overcame me that night. I could not move my legs, my arms, my hands. I thought to take Hashem's dagger or one of his pebbles even, but every time I thought what I would do, I found my limbs bound."

Odelia considered the words. Was she telling the truth?

"I know it sounds as if I am making excuses. I hate how weak I was in that moment. Please, believe that I would never want such a horrible thing to befall you. And as for me wanting Aden, you have my word I will not pursue him. I vowed it to myself that very next day."

"But I saw you in his tent."

"I was passing by, and he asked for water."

Odelia sighed. Playing judge did not settle well with her. She could not see Sherah's heart—only Adonai could. Would she forever hold this resentment toward the woman she had made a covenant with? And what were the meaning and power of covenants if one broke them whenever they wished? If one decided the keeping of such a promise was too difficult?

"I believe you," Odelia said softly.

Sherah raised hope-filled eyes to her. "You do?"

Odelia nodded. "I also found my limbs useless that night. I felt I was not myself, not a part of my own body."

Sherah bit her lip. "I know I do not have a right to ask, but I am sorry for my actions—or lack of—that night. Regret has been my constant companion, and I cannot fathom a time it will not be. I beg of you to forgive me."

She had expected Sherah to make excuses or brush her off. But this unexpected openness caused fresh waves of emotion to tunnel through Odelia. Her chest expanded with bittersweet sadness, but something else as well—hope.

"We made a covenant of sisters. Now that Zillah has left us, it is just us. I cannot hold unforgiveness toward you, Sherah. I do forgive you."

As soon as the words left her mouth, it was as if a floodgate of bright light filled her insides. As if she'd carried a donkey's pack upon her own back and the words had released her of the burden.

But she knew it wasn't only her words. It was Adonai. Somehow, though she was not in the temple and though a priest did not intercede for her, His Spirit touched her being. Somehow, perhaps, He was paving the way of faith for her.

Tentatively at first, Sherah folded her arms around Odelia. They sobbed together. Not only for all they'd been through with the attack but for the loss of Zillah as well, the continued grief of leaving their homes and loved ones.

"I miss Zillah," Sherah said on the last wobbly ebb of her tears.

"I do too."

"She was the only friend who would put up with me. She told me hard truths when I needed to hear them. That is not an easy thing to do with a stubborn woman like me."

They laughed, and it felt wonderful.

Odelia pulled back from the embrace. "If you need someone to tell you hard truths, I may be up to the task."

Sherah's eyes shone through her tears. "Yes, please."

"You have no business baking bread any longer. It is hard as flint."

Sherah smiled. "I am all too willing to hand the task over. In return, I will sew your robe. The torn places are a disgrace to style."

Odelia smiled, staring at the flames eating up the kindling they'd gathered from the wadi. They sat in silence, the tension in the air growing more somber as Odelia worked up the courage to speak what was on her mind.

"The night of the attack, Aden asked me to be his wife."

Sherah's eyes widened, but Odelia did not see a hint of jealousy in their depths. "That is good. I am happy for you, my sister."

Odelia smiled. "Thank you. He will be the high priest. I am struggling to accept this."

"Why on earth would you struggle over such a prestigious position? The wife of the high priest—what honor!"

"I feel undeserving."

Sherah reached for her hand and squeezed. "Then perhaps you are exactly where Adonai prefers you to be."

Odelia stared at her friend, unraveling her words, when Hashem approached their fire at a run, his breaths heaving. "Odelia!"

Odelia grabbed her bag. "What is it? Is someone hurt?"

Hashem drew to a stop, an impish grin on his face. "No, Aden wishes to speak to you."

She let out a gusty breath. "Is that all?"

Sherah gave her a friendly jostle. "Is that all? That man cannot get enough of you! Here, let me straighten your head covering." She reached to adjust Odelia's crooked headscarf.

"Thank you."

"Now go see what need that man has for you."

Hashem rolled his eyes. "Women," he muttered, shaking his head and strolling to the next campfire to be with some of the other boys.

CHAPTER EIGHTEEN

Odelia walked to Aden's camp, the words he'd recited still swirling in her mind, her reconciliation with Sherah light in her chest.

Aden's tent was near Eliashib's, the two campsites closest to the Kohlit hill and the temple treasures. He sat poking at his fire.

"Shalom," Odelia called.

Aden looked up, a small skin of barley beer at his side that the boys from Ein Gedi had brought back with them earlier that day. "Shalom, Odelia. Thank you for coming."

She bowed. "My lord."

He waved a hand at her. "Enough of that." He raised the skin of beer. "Would you like some?"

"I will have a little." She removed her sandals and sat on the far end of his mat, arranging her frayed robe around herself, careful to hide the worst of the tearing that Sherah had pointed out.

He handed her a flask of the beer, and she took small sips in order to strain the hulls that drifted to the top.

"That boy has some remarkable questions."

Her lips twitched. "You mean Hashem."

He nodded.

"He has amazed me since I first met him."

"Sick with fever at the city walls, did you not say?"

"Yes."

"For a Gentile, he is certainly knowledgeable of the Torah."

"He spent a lot of time with Shaphan." She bit her lip. "Shaphan did not consider him a Gentile. Hashem willingly took up the sign of circumcision to identify with our people."

Aden's brows raised. "A big decision for one so young."

"A decision made without coercion."

Aden poked the fire with a stick. "That may explain his enthusiasm for the Torah and Jeremiah's scrolls. We had a lengthy conversation. His mind is sharp. I am looking forward to teaching him."

"He would very much like that, I am sure. You will teach all the boys, will you not?"

He nodded. "And I have not forgotten my promise to teach you to read either."

She fidgeted with the edge of the straw mat. "You have much to think about. My literacy is not of utmost importance."

Aden sighed. "Odelia."

She met his gaze but could not hold it for long.

"I am sorry the scroll upset you."

Heat that had nothing to do with her proximity to the fire billowed over her. "I did not intend to make a spectacle of myself."

"You did not. I am simply...aware of you. Whether you wish to run from me or not, you are my wife."

A hammering began in her chest. She ached to look into those eyes, to allow him to see her—really see her—but she could not. It would only cause them both more pain in the end.

She moved to stand. "Forgive me for my display. Will that be all?"

"Please, do not leave. I have much to discuss."

She swallowed, vacillating between the warm mat beside Aden and the relative safety of the fire at the mouth of the women's cave. The call of a bleating sheep sounded in the distance.

"I am tired. Perhaps we best save our discussions for the light of morning when my mind is fresh."

"I am helping the boys build a wood hut for the animals tomorrow. Please. Will you sit?"

She lowered herself to the mat again, forgoing the grace with which she sat the first time.

"It is okay to feel emotional over Jeremiah's words. But remember, you do not share your abba's heart."

"Only the same blood." Her words came out with a bitter tinge that soaked her lips with their acrid taste.

"Did you not just tell me that Hashem is Hebrew through and through—not because of his blood but because of his spirit?"

He was intelligent enough to twist her words back to herself, wasn't he? "Yes."

"Then is it unreasonable to see that you are a child of the El Shaddai, not because of your blood but because of your heart?"

She cleared her throat. "Is this the matter you so urgently need to discuss with me?"

She felt him staring at her, hesitating before sitting back from the fire and spreading his legs in front of him. "I suppose not. I am a bit embarrassed to tell you that Hashem's questions shook me up."

She couldn't stop the smile that came to her face. "The boy has a way of getting beneath our pretenses, does he not?"

Aden grunted. "You know I respect your counsel. I realize your abba has been heavy on your mind, especially given this night. I have thought of mine also—the abba I have on earth, that is."

Baruch. Was it fair to compare Pashhur, the unfaithful priest, with Baruch, scribe to Jeremiah?

"You are worried for him."

"Yes. More than that, I feel a weight of responsibility."

"For the well-being of your abba?"

"Not exactly." He shifted in his seat. "If Jeremiah and my abba were taken to Babylon as I assume they were, then they will give the latter part of the scroll to our people there. They will bring the message of hope. It might be what gets Adonai's people through the next sixty years."

She searched the crevice of each nuance and syllable to find meaning behind them. Slowly, understanding dawned on her, simmering between them like a pot of water to boil.

"And if they were not taken to Babylon…"

The corners of his mouth pulled downward. "That is what worries me."

What a strange state of things, that Aden should be anxious over his abba not making it to the city of their conquerors. And yet, it was their only way to salvation.

"I am certain the conquering army has kept them safe. You yourself said that King Nebuchadnezzar favored Jeremiah for urging the last of Jerusalem's four kings to surrender to him. He will be cared for."

"If they were found alive when the army came into the royal palace, I am sure that will be the case."

Odelia inhaled a slight breath. "You fear King Zedekiah had them killed before then?"

He swallowed, his throat bobbing decisively. "I do not see what motivation he would have, but I cannot rule it out either."

"I understand your concern, but I also think you worry for nothing."

He met her gaze. "I pray it is so. But if it is not… If Jeremiah and my abba and the copies of their scroll were destroyed in the taking of the city…I may be responsible for one day getting the scroll to Babylon. For getting its message to our people."

"Oh my." She allowed the idea to soak through to the marrow of her bones. "Surely word will come eventually. Or perhaps we can send Jehoahaz or one of the others to discover if your abba has survived?"

"Perhaps." But he didn't sound at peace with the idea.

"We will have to better brace ourselves next time Hashem asks a question, will we not?" Odelia tried to lighten the heaviness clinging to Aden's cozy fire.

He smiled. "I thought you would have given me fairer warning about the brute."

She laughed. Two times in one night. Did that mean there was hope for healing?

"I have not been much help."

"But you have. You assured me my worries are useless. I suppose we have sixty years to get the message of hope to Babylon, to our people."

"I pray to Adonai it will not be that long."

"As do I."

They sat in companionable silence for a few moments before Odelia stood. "I should be returning."

He did not move to stand but instead craned his neck up to her. "You know, someday soon we will have to speak of our future."

She closed her eyes. Why, though? Why could they not go on like this, exchanging thoughts, pretending their last conversation hadn't happened?

"I know," she whispered before taking her leave.

CHAPTER NINETEEN

When Odelia spotted Aden approaching the women's fire two weeks later, she tucked her head and concentrated all her efforts on weaving the basket in her lap. Not until he spoke to her, his sandaled feet in view of her gaze, did she halt her task.

"Odelia, may I speak with you?"

She shared a knowing look with Sherah, who sat beside her, before laying aside her unfinished basket. "Of course."

She fell in step beside Aden, acknowledging that something stiff and rigid hung between them. They had not spoken much of late, and yet they could not stay betrothed forever. The high priest needed a wife.

She kept up with his brisk steps. They walked past the tents and the animal pen, past the dry wadis and the clay oven. Then past the Kohlit hill. Thinking of the ark, a fierce longing welled within her. The temple had offered safety and security. She missed bowing her head to the marble floor, feeling its coolness against her forehead and nose, reciting the many prayers of her childhood and always adding in some of her own. She longed for Shaphan's steady presence, his grandfatherly smile.

She wanted that familiar safety, that place of comfort.

But the mercy seat was deep within a cave she was not allowed to enter. Had it been Adonai she had turned to for comfort all these years, all those visits to the temple, or had it been the sheer building—the gorgeous beauty of what Solomon had built? The gold, the marble, the ornamental wood?

She pulled her mantle more tightly around herself and followed Aden as he climbed one of the nearby hills. Dust and pebbles wedged between her toes and the worn leather of her sandals. Why was he taking her to the top of a hill?

When they reached the highest point, she bent over, out of breath atop the dusty mound. Nothing but open sky above them. Dust coated her lips, but she closed her eyes against it. Here, Aden would surely say what he needed to say.

"It is time." Aden looked down the hill toward their little settlement.

"Time?" A single drop of cool rain landed on her head.

"For you to come into my tent. We cannot pretend any longer."

She worked her tongue around in her mouth. How she wanted to jump at the opportunity, but doubt held her back. "Are you certain?"

He faced her, reaching for her hands. "I care for you, Odelia. Yes, your faith drew me to you, but if it was real, and I sense it was, it has not disappeared even if you don't feel it as acutely."

She forced down the emotion working its way up her body at the beautiful words. Beautiful, impossible words. "You do not understand, Aden. You do not—"

"I understand you have been avoiding our betrothal, and I have allowed you to. But no longer. We are husband and wife, and I will not stand by any longer while you push me away. I have spoken to Eliashib, and he does not disagree with my intentions to see our marriage through to completion."

She bit her lip, hard. Raindrops soaked through the sleeves of her mantle, chilling her to the bone. "My imma," she choked out.

He tilted his head to the side. "What of your imma?"

"She worshiped other gods. Ba'al and the queen of heaven. Sometimes I wonder if she influenced my abba. I fear…"

"You fear that you will be like your imma?"

"And bring judgment upon you and our people. You are to be the high priest, Aden. How can Adonai approve of Pashhur's daughter, a woman who has doubts enough of her own, as your wife?"

The words lay between them, naked and exposed, taunting the future he claimed for them.

She could not look at him. Not now with her fears so exposed.

"I am sorry." Still, she looked to the ground. The rain fell around them, soaking her through. Her insides pulled tight as a bowstring around his silence. She wound her arms in front of herself. "Now you understand. You understand why I cannot be your wife."

"I understand nothing of the sort."

She raised her gaze to him. The rain turned to a gentle mist, a wedge of sunlight peering through the clouds on the horizon.

He reached a hand to her face, ran a thumb along her cheek as he'd done before. "Beloved, we've been over this. Do you think I do not have doubts about Adonai's love? Do you think my faith is always unshakable? No, dear one. It is not the size of our faith that is of import. It is Who we are placing our faith in that matters. Adonai is the faithful one."

Adonai is the faithful one.

The words shimmered within her, calling her to a hope greater than herself.

"Adam failed, beloved. Abraham failed, Moses failed, King David failed. But Adonai did not fail. He has called us into His story—a story that is not always beautiful but a story that always leaves space for restoration and forgiveness."

"For restoration and forgiveness…" Her strained whisper barely reached her own ears.

"And even if your faith fails, I will be there to point you back to Adonai. Because that's what love does. And make no mistake, Odelia. I love you."

Something let loose in her chest, a lightness replacing the tangled mass of fear that had lodged there for weeks.

"We will learn together. You, me, and Hashem."

She buried her face in her hands. She did not deserve such goodness, such generosity.

He ran a thumb along her jaw. "I was an orphan, but when my abba and imma took me in, they showed me a love that went beyond blood. Looking back, I wonder if Adonai was not preparing me for this time all along. I have no doubts on this, my love."

She shivered with the cold wetness of her tunic, with the possibility of what Aden offered.

"We are not the same people who left Jerusalem. We have been through much and are learning to be gracious with one another. We are learning to love as Adonai does. You have nothing to fear."

She bit her lip to keep sobs from escaping.

"I wish to spread my garment over you, Odelia. Will you allow me?" He unfastened his robe, and when she nodded, he threw it around her shivering frame, drawing her closer.

"Are you certain?"

He silenced her with the press of his finger to her lips. "More than certain."

"I will fail."

"As will I. And then we will forgive and start again, looking to Adonai."

She nodded, smiling through her tears. When Aden lowered his mouth to hers, she sank into the warmth of his lips, the solid security of his embrace.

She could have kissed him forever, just the two of them alone on this hill, the camp far below, nothing but his breath between them. When he finally pulled away, he groaned lightly. "Fortunate for me our thirty days of betrothal are up. Please say we can continue with our ceremony."

Odelia laughed softly. "I pray you do not regret this decision."

He ran his hands up and down her arms. "Regret marrying the most captivating woman I have ever known? I do not see how that is possible, *ahuvati*."

Oh, but she did not deserve this man.

His gaze wandered over her shoulder, and he smiled, gently turning her and pointing into the sky. "Look."

She gasped at the brilliance of the bow arching over the sky, vibrant colors cast over their heads from one end of the horizon to the other.

"It is the most beautiful thing I have ever seen," she whispered, her eyes soaking up the display of colors.

"Adonai is spreading His covering over us." The sure baritone of his voice danced through the air. She leaned into him, and he pulled her tight against his broad chest. "We should get back and announce the news. And warm you by the fire. I do not need my wife falling ill before I bring her into our marriage bed."

Her skin warmed at the words. Hand in hand, they returned to camp. When they announced the news, Sherah danced around her, planning how she might arrange her hair for the ceremony the next day.

"Did I miss something?" Hashem returned from an unsuccessful hunt in the middle of Sherah's prancing.

"Odelia and Aden are to be married tomorrow!"

"Also, Aden will be anointed as high priest very soon." Odelia studied the boy.

Since the attack, he'd become adept at hiding his feelings, but she did not miss the slight panic in his eyes. "That is good."

"Aden wishes for you to be a part of our family, Hashem."

The boy blinked, fast. "He—he does?"

Odelia smiled. "It was one of the first things he said when offering to spread his garment over me. That you should be with us as well."

"I—I will be in the family of the high priest?"

Odelia couldn't contain her laughter. How completely unexpected that this Gentile boy whom her abba had deemed unworthy to enter his house would now call Aden his abba. "It would seem so."

He lunged forward, wrapping his arms around her waist. When he pulled away, he swiped at his face. "Poxy on these womanly tears!" he called out with relish, causing Odelia and Sherah to laugh again.

It wasn't until later that night by the warmth of the fire with just Odelia and Hashem that the boy spoke again. "I am glad we will be family, but I already thought of you as my sister. I am grateful for you."

"You have grown much over these last months. I wish you could have stayed a child a bit longer." Not that the boy ever had much of a childhood to begin with. Not like her, running carefree through the tunnels of Jerusalem.

He let his hands fall over his knees, clasped them slightly before him. "Aden is a good man."

"Yes, he is."

"Like Shaphan, not like…"

Odelia bit her bottom lip but couldn't bring herself to finish Hashem's sentence out loud. *Like her abba.* "Yes, like Shaphan."

Serious dark eyes studied her before dropping to the dirt. "I am not like Shaphan."

Odelia lifted her hand to his dark locks. "What do you mean?"

His face grew red. "I have murder in my heart."

She swallowed, praying for wisdom. "I do not have answers, Hashem. But I know only Adonai can mend our bruised hearts." She remembered Aden's words. "Adonai is the faithful one. We must only keep looking toward Him."

The boy's mouth twitched. "Thank you, Odelia. This will be a new beginning for us, will it not?"

She smiled, bringing him close. "Yes."

"I never thought I would be a son."

Odelia smiled. "Perhaps Adonai is granting all of us a second chance."

CHAPTER TWENTY

Aden's anointing ceremony was held without much fanfare, the amber liquid from the horn of oil dripping over his head in a symbol of promise after Eliashib had put the priestly tunic and sash upon him. Aden laid his hands on the head of a spotless goat and Eliashib slaughtered it, spreading its blood on their altar and burning its fat and internal organs at the mouth of the Kohlit cave, thereby presenting Aden before the Lord. He did the same with a ram, dabbing its blood on the lobe of Aden's right ear, the thumb of his right hand, and the big toe of his right foot. After all the sacrifices were given, including the wave offering of bread with olive oil, Aden ate the meat and the bread, concluding his induction as high priest before Yahweh.

The next day, Odelia bathed in the Salt Sea after offering her own sacrifices. Then, with all watching, Aden draped the end of his robe over Odelia's shoulders and promised to love and care for her all their days on earth. Her husband's gentle touch in their lantern-lit bridal tent, smelling of cinnamon and juniper, melted away her fears and doubts. Though she'd agonized over her lagging faith the last several weeks, in the light of Aden's love, she saw hope for the future.

With the ceremonies over and Aden tending to the ark and the temple treasures with Eliashib's help, quiet contentment settled over their group. Aden began to teach Odelia and Hashem to read. Both excelled, and after several weeks, were reading bits and pieces of the scrolls Aden kept stored in his tent. His patient way with both her and Hashem, the care he demonstrated in building a relationship with the boy, served to grow her love for him tenfold.

Perhaps that was how one was to view Adonai's love as well. To dwell on it and gaze on it and meditate on it until it bloomed and overflowed in one's own heart, like a spring wildflower.

Steady autumn rains began to fall, filling their cistern. More stone ovens were built, as well as the foundation of mud-brick homes. Their town was taking root.

The day after Odelia managed to read an entire page in the scroll of Jeremiah for herself, Jehoahaz pounded into their small village upon a new mount. He had purchased the stallion on his last trip to Ein Gedi and had taken long trips, trying to gather what news he could of the besieged Jerusalem and her people.

The cloud of dust created by his chestnut horse billowed into the sky, and Odelia straightened from where she used a pestle to grind grains of wheat in a clay bowl. Jehoahaz slipped off his mount. Sherah dropped her task of carding wool to meet her brother, and he placed a hand on the sleeve of her robe and spoke something to her then turned and strode to Odelia and Aden's cave.

"I must speak with you both."

Odelia nodded. "Aden is in Kohlit." When not making the sacrifices, Aden spent long hours in the cave, praying for their small community and for their people exiled in Babylon. Though Aden had been hesitant to take upon the mantle of priest, Adonai had given him the strength to step into his role within the community with grace and enthusiasm. "He will emerge before the evening meal."

Jehoahaz paced. "Very well. I will wait."

Odelia's chest tightened. What did Jehoahaz learn on his trip? Part of her wanted to sink into this new life and her new marriage—the new family she would build. She would never forget their people, of course, and she knew Aden was especially troubled by their suffering, but Adonai had led them here. They were taking care of the ark of the testimony. In time, He would show them the way forward.

She continued to grind the wheat, pounding it until it turned soft in the clay bowl before repeating the process. When Aden finally emerged from the cave, the look of peace on his face turned to concern when he spotted Jehoahaz pacing back and forth beside Odelia not far from their tent.

Aden rushed over, his priestly garments and ephod left behind in the cave and replaced with his ordinary robe. He greeted Jehoahaz. "Brother, you have brought news?"

Jehoahaz nodded, and Odelia noticed a tic starting in his left eye. "I have." His gaze flicked to Odelia. "Perhaps we should walk."

"Whatever you tell me will not be a secret for long," Aden said. "We have been expecting the worst, I am afraid. Please, Brother. Do not keep us in suspense."

"I have already spoken to my men and to Eliashib. It is as we have feared. Judah is now a vassal province of the Babylonian empire. Jerusalem is no more. Regiments are scouring the city, taking inventory of the temple treasures left behind."

Though Odelia had seen the evidence of her burning city with her own eyes, the words from Jehoahaz's mouth carved out a piece of her heart, leaving it for the carrion birds to feast upon.

Grief washed over her with fresh vigor, and she bowed her head in silent mourning for their beloved city.

Finally, Aden spoke. "Jeremiah told as much. We saw the destruction. Nevertheless, it is shocking and sad to hear."

"There is surprising news as well. News I would doubt myself if my source was not so reputable." Jehoahaz shifted where he stood, the worn leather of his boots showing a hole in one side. Would they have enough supplies once the coldness of winter crept in?

Jehoahaz continued. "King Nebuchadnezzar appointed a governor in the land of Judah at Mizpah to oversee those remaining in the land."

Odelia's legs weakened, no stronger than mutton jelly. "We are not the only remnant?"

The soldier shook his head. "We are not. Nebuchadnezzar has allowed men, women, and children from the poorest in the land to remain in Judah."

Odelia's head swirled. The poorest of the poor to be stewards of their land for the next sixty years.

"Who has the king appointed governor?"

Jehoahaz's lips twitched. "Gedaliah ben Ahikam."

Odelia's mouth fell open. Shaphan's grandson. Son of the very man who had spared Jeremiah after her abba punished him. Miracle of miracles.

Adonai, is this the beginning of our restoration?

Aden let out what could only be described as a joyful noise—part laugh, part disbelief. In the next instant, however, he grew serious. "How reliable is this news?"

"I would stake my life on it. I met Johanan ben Kareah, a loyal friend from childhood on his way to Mizpah to serve Gedaliah. He would not lie about such a thing. Even if he intended to, I am not certain he could imagine such an impossible story."

"If this is true, then we may go to join the others in Mizpah." Odelia searched her husband's face. "We can live in peace under Gedaliah and not live in fear of Nebuchadnezzar if he himself appointed Gedaliah as governor."

Was this their way forward? The earthenware jar Aden had brought to Secacah? Was this how Jeremiah's prophecy of their people again owning land in Judah would come true?

Aden held up his hand. "We must proceed with caution. It is not only our lives at risk but the well-being of the ark. While our flesh wants to reunite with our people, we must consider every unturned stone of potential danger and seek wisdom."

"Johanan would not lie to me. He is like a brother." Jehoahaz crossed his arms in front of his chest, his mood threatening to turn surly.

"I believe you, Brother."

"There is something else."

Aden nodded his encouragement.

"The prophet Jeremiah is with Gedaliah at Mizpah. As is your abba and the king's daughters."

Aden blinked, his knees visibly weakening. "Truly?"

Jehoahaz smiled, his previous churlish mood evaporating. "King Nebuchadnezzar's captain of the guard allowed Jeremiah the choice between accompanying the exiles to Babylon or joining the company at Mizpah. Jeremiah chose the latter. It is not surprising that your abba chose to stay with him, faithful to the end."

Odelia blinked. If Jeremiah willingly stayed with Gedaliah, then a copy of his scroll must have been sent to Babylon with the exiles. Certainly, he wouldn't have stayed without assuring the people of a future hope?

Jehoahaz clasped Aden's shoulder. "Gedaliah is continuing with the counsel of Jeremiah, advising the people who remain to serve the Chaldeans, to not be afraid of their captors but to serve the king of Babylon. They are seeing to the harvests and dwelling in the cities that need tending."

Odelia could almost taste the abundance of summer fruits—something they did not have in Secacah. Oh, but surely now that Gedaliah had been promised peace, they could travel to Mizpah and enjoy the last days of the harvest with their people! She could meet the prophet Jeremiah and fall at his feet for the sins of her abba. She could meet her father-in-law.

But what of the ark? Surely it would honor Adonai to hand the care of it over to Jeremiah. Would he approve of all they'd done to spare it? Would it be safe in the occupied land? So many questions Jehoahaz's news had brought them!

"This is a lot to take in." Aden turned, staring off toward the horizon, northwest, toward Mizpah. "Of course, there is nothing I want more than to run toward Mizpah, to see my abba and introduce my wife to him. To see Jeremiah and talk over everything that has happened, to enjoy a harvest." He turned back toward them. "But we must pray. We were placed as caretakers over the ark and the treasures. That is our first duty."

"But Jeremiah himself said the ark would not be remembered, that a new covenant was coming. Perhaps this is the beginning of that." Odelia wrung her hands.

"I will seek out Eliashib. We will pray." He reached for Odelia. "I will not be partaking in dinner tonight. I am going to return to the cave."

She nodded, probing his troubled eyes with her own. "No matter what we decide, this is good news. Your abba and Jeremiah are alive. Adonai has answered our prayers."

His gaze softened, revealing the hazel flecks in his eyes. He kissed her head. "You are right, my wife. Thank you for reminding me."

"I will pray throughout the night with you."

He kissed her softly, this time on the mouth, before he departed. Odelia longed to go with him, but they'd been adhering to the Law—she was not to enter the cave, as it was considered the Holy Place. Sighing, she meandered down the hill toward the tents. After a simple meal of bread, figs, and cheese with Hashem, she slipped into their tent and burrowed beneath her blanket.

She lay still, listening to the distant sounds of the night—fires crackling, quiet laughter, a child crying. Shifting, she knelt on the ground and prayed, ruminating first on Adonai's compassion and love. She always started there, reminding herself of this one simple truth. It served to quell any doubts, to anchor her in the love of the Lord.

A peaceful quiet descended upon Odelia. She could not enter the cave, just as she couldn't enter the Holy Place in the temple in

Jerusalem. Again, she was locked out. But here and now she felt certain Adonai heard her. He had promised a new covenant—a covenant bound by the Spirit of God and a person's heart. Almost as if he called her to be a temple, a dwelling place for the Lord.

Was such a thought sacrilege?

Adonai, grant us wisdom. Light the path forward—the path You would have us take that honors You.

She fell asleep with her head bowed to the ground. When Aden came in, before the sun began to rise, she stirred. He disrobed, sliding beneath the blankets beside her in his undertunic and reaching for her.

"I tried to stay awake praying with you," she murmured.

He kissed her, pulling her close. "I felt your prayers."

She blinked, more awake now. "You did?"

"Yes. You were my Aaron and Hur, helping to hold up my arms as they did for Moses."

"I do not think Aaron and Hur fell asleep."

He chuckled. She snuggled deeper into his arms, inhaling the cypress scent of him mixed with the heady incense used in the Holy Place.

He trailed his finger down her bare arm. "I have prayed and spoken with Eliashib. We agree I should go to my abba."

Her heart leaped. "I cannot wait to meet him."

An imperceptible shift in the air between them, a slight tenseness to his muscles alerted her to the words that would come. "I must go by myself."

It was not her place to argue. She must respect her husband and his decisions. But then she remembered her own imma, who buried her head in the making of bread dough or the worshiping of the queen of heaven while staying quiet when her abba threw Hashem out of the house or came home with news of a betrothal to Adino.

But that was not fair. Aden was not Abba.

And neither was she Imma. Still…

"Please let me go with you," she begged. "I am your wife, and my rightful place is by your side. There is no reason for me to stay while you conduct all the important affairs of Adonai."

Aden laughed softly. "Is that what visiting my abba is?"

"You know there is more to it than that. I fear you are ashamed of me."

He lifted himself onto one elbow. "Odelia, you know that is not true."

"My abba's deeds will follow me all the days of my life, will they not?"

She heard herself acting like a petulant child, and yet she could not stop the words pouring from her mouth.

By the faint light of the moon, she saw his jaw soften. "My wife, I can only tell you so many times that who your abba is does not matter to me. I am not convinced it matters to Adonai. What more can I say?"

She gritted her teeth, silent.

"I fear for your safety on such a trip. That is why I do not think you should accompany me." He threw the covers off himself and pulled on his tunic.

Her stomach lurched. Regret gnawed at her innards. "Where are you going?"

"I think perhaps I need to pray more."

"Please forgive me, Husband. I should not have spoken so carelessly."

He planted a kiss on her head. "You are forgiven. I will see you in the morning, beloved."

She watched the tent flap envelop him and then close, leaving her in lonely silence again. She groaned, flopping back on the pallet, remorse nipping at her insides. Had she learned nothing of Aden's love that she must push to test him further?

Sleep eluded her for some time before she finally succumbed to it. She dreamed of traveling with Aden, but not toward Mizpah—rather into the Holy of Holies. Together, they approached Adonai's mercy seat, the Shekinah glimmering around them. A whispered knowing traveled over her, as if Yahweh Himself was binding her to her husband, commissioning her for something she did not yet understand.

She awoke with a gasp, her eyes wide in the dusky predawn light. She glanced at Aden, back beneath their blanket, awake and staring at her.

"You came back," she whispered.

"I will always come back."

She rubbed her head. "I had a dream…"

"As did I."

"We were in the temple, together."

He blinked. "Yes."

"You dreamed the same?"

He nodded.

"What does it mean?"

"I think you must accompany me to Mizpah."

CHAPTER TWENTY-ONE

Odelia hugged Hashem to her, noting the new muscles in his still-skinny frame. "Do not grow too fast while we are gone."

"I should come along. Aden is no good with a slingshot."

Aden laughed. "True, dear boy. Very true. And yet, the horse would not be able to carry all three of us, and we do not wish to linger. I am hopeful there will be a next time."

Odelia eyed Jehoahaz's chestnut stallion, packed light with two skins of water, a loaf of fresh bread hot from the stone ovens, a bit of cheese, a cooked partridge, two blankets, and the scrolls of Jeremiah. If they rode steadily, they would make it to Mizpah by the end of the next day.

Hashem firmed his jaw and gave a decisive nod.

Aden tousled his hair and leaned down, speaking in low tones. "Between the two of us, Jehoahaz is not that skilled with a slingshot either. He needs all the help he can get to protect our village and the ark."

"Whoa, now." Jehoahaz and Sherah strode up to them. "Is this how one repays a friend who allows him to borrow his finest possession?" The stallion nuzzled Jehoahaz's hand as he leaned to place his face near the beast's.

Aden laughed, and the two men shook hands while Sherah threw her arms around Odelia. "I will miss you," Sherah whispered beside Odelia's headscarf.

"I will miss you also," Odelia said, noting the wholehearted truthfulness of the words. The woman had changed. Then again, so had Odelia. No longer did she call Sherah *sister* out of a covenant obligation, she called her *sister* out of her heart's desire.

After Odelia had bid Eliana goodbye, she accepted Aden's help to climb onto the stallion. He flung himself up behind her, cradling her in the cavity of his arms as he grabbed for the reins.

Jehoahaz gave his horse one last pat on the neck and looked at Odelia. "Take good care of him."

Odelia patted Aden on the arm. "I will."

The soldier gave her a wry grin. "I meant my horse."

Aden smirked. "Of course you did. Farewell, my brother. We will not tarry long."

They started away, and Odelia inhaled the sulfurous scent of the Salt Sea, wondering how long it would take before she could no longer smell the aroma that had come to symbolize home for her.

When they'd ridden more than a mile, Aden turned the stallion around so they might have a last glimpse of the goat-hair tents and foundations of mud-brick houses in their small village, the sea glimmering behind it in an impressive backdrop of azure beauty. He breathed a prayer over the inhabitants.

"It has come to feel like home, has it not?" she said.

He nodded. "In some ways, yes. But I have a feeling that wherever you land will be home to me." He squeezed her to himself, and she turned her body so she could kiss him as they sat atop the beast.

"I could get used to this type of traveling," he murmured. "It is a bit more pleasant than hiding out in tunnels."

They rode steadily for the next hour before Aden slowed and dismounted beneath a terebinth tree growing beside a trickling river. He led the stallion to drink as Odelia stretched her legs and washed some of the dust of the ride from her eyes and face.

After she had freshened herself, she leaned against the bark of the tree and closed her eyes, moaning with pleasure. "I could listen to the sound of running water forever and never become sick of it."

"It does not make you feel as if you have to relieve yourself?"

Her eyes flew open. "Aden!" But she couldn't stop the giggle that escaped. "Are priests supposed to have such humor?"

He shrugged, his eyes twinkling as he dug in their pack and handed her an *emmer* cracker. "I never claimed to be your typical priest." He lowered himself to lean against the tree and tore a piece of bread with his teeth. "I hope Jeremiah is pleased with how we have conducted our affairs."

"How could he not be?"

He chewed with care. "I find it hard to believe the symbol of our faith should be stored away in a cave for any extended time."

"It is temporary, is it not? We are keeping it safe until it can be returned to the Holy City."

"Until then, we keep the ark in a cave for sixty years?"

She placed a hand on his arm. "I cannot pretend to have answers, my husband. But you and Eliashib sought Adonai's wisdom. We have all done the best we knew how. Shaphan trusted you when he appointed you on this mission. None of us could have foreseen the murder of so many of our priests."

"Which brings me to another troubling thought."

"You did not have to wait until we are miles away from Secacah to voice your doubts to me."

He smiled. "I suppose not. But there is something about being in the middle of the wilderness with only you and me that prods me to speak my heart."

She warmed beneath his words.

He bit into a cracker. "I am not certain Adonai occupies the ark any longer."

She straightened. "Why do you say so?" He had voiced his doubt before but never with so much certainty.

"I have spent hours in the cave praying, and while I believe Yahweh has not abandoned the ark altogether, I cannot say I sense His presence greater in that cave than I do outside of it." He winced. "I pray this is not sacrilege. Perhaps I am no better a priest than the ones in Jerusalem that the Lord condemned. And yet is that not what Jeremiah foretold? That the Law that had been housed in the ark would ultimately be housed in the hearts of His people? If He was not bound at Shiloh and no longer in Jerusalem, perhaps He will reveal Himself anywhere for His people in worship and prayer."

"Aden, Adonai knows your heart. He knows your struggles." She bit her lip, choosing her next words with care. "You once told me it is not the size of our faith but the object of our faith that is of worth. Perhaps in the same way, it is not so much a matter of where He resides but that we are faithful in serving Him and seeking Him out. If He wants to reveal the place of His presence to us, we must trust He will."

He gazed at her as if she were an intricate tapestry.

Her skin burned beneath his intense perusal. "What is it?"

"When I dreamed you should come along with me, I had no idea it might be for this very moment. For I am not sure I could have heard what you just said amid all my priestly duties. Adonai knew I needed you to show me His grace."

"Grace," she whispered. "'The Lord, the Lord, the compassionate and gracious God...'" She quoted part of the verse from the book of Exodus, as it overflowed from her heart. The Lord beginning to define to His people who He himself was.

"Thank Adonai that His Law is meant to be molded by grace. Without it, I am not certain I could be a priest at all, let alone a priest serving in the Holy of Holies."

"Then I would say you are in the perfect position to do so." She bestowed on him an encouraging smile, which he matched with one of his own. He crawled closer and kissed her long and deep.

She wrapped his arms around him. "I have been thinking about our ancestor Jacob and his dream of the stairway to heaven."

Aden murmured acknowledgment, encouraging her to continue.

"That place was an opening to heaven, was it not? A place where the heavy curtain that blocks us from God's courts was peeled back?"

"Yes, I suppose it was. But since then we have had the ark and the temple to serve as that thin place, to serve as our place of communion with Yahweh."

She sat quietly, fingering the hem of her robe. "But there is a new covenant to come. Perhaps, with a new thin place—a new gate to heaven. A way for Adonai to peel back the curtain."

"That is a worthy thought, and I pray it is so. No matter what awaits us in Mizpah, I pray Adonai's spirit goes with us."

"I as well." She couldn't explain it, but day by day Adonai had sown seeds of faith in her own heart. At first, they were tiny and vulnerable, like a mustard seed. But they had grown and faced challenges. Been battered by harsh weather and the storms of life. Aden's love for her had served to water her faith, to testify to Adonai's goodness. Now, she felt it growing like the tree by this beautiful stream.

And it was all Adonai's doing.

They prayed together before consulting the map Jehoahaz had given them and then climbed back on the stallion to ride until the sun began to round its descent in the sky. They made camp in a rocky outcropping of brush and stone and started out early the next day until finally, the village of Mizpah stood before them.

They were still a distance from the city when a rider came tearing across the green and fertile plains. Odelia had just begun to enjoy the luscious grasslands, breathing in the fresh air, so unlike the arid conditions of what they knew near the Salt Sea at Secacah.

Aden pulled on the reins. "They must be on watch with the governor here."

The rider, adorned in a soldier's attire, pulled up several cubits before them. Aden dismounted, holding the reins with one hand and raising his other hand in greeting.

"Shalom!"

The soldier nodded. "Shalom. State your name and your purpose in visiting Mizpah."

"I am Aden ben Baruch and this is my wife, Odelia. Jehoahaz ben Aziel told us about the governorship run here under King Nebuchadnezzar. We hope to see my abba and the prophet Jeremiah."

The soldier's eyes softened at the mention of Jehoahaz. "It did not take my friend long to report the news." He dipped his head. "I am Johanan ben Kareah."

One corner of Aden's mouth crept upward. "It is good to be among friends."

Johanan turned his mount toward the town. "I am certain you are anxious to see your abba, but I do have orders to take all visitors straight to Gedaliah."

"Of course."

Odelia's tense muscles melted beneath the order of this place, beneath the simple yet welcoming sight of smoke rising from courtyard ovens. The scent of fresh-baked bread and simmering stews. While Secacah had blessed her in many ways, it often felt like constant survival. Here, it seemed, people were living. No doubt it was beneath a heavy grief, and yet it spoke of a normalcy she hadn't known since before the siege, maybe even before the first deportation of her people at the hand of the Babylonians.

The soldier led them into the town. Everywhere Odelia looked, date palms and olive trees thrived. Wildflowers spattered the distant hills and the patches of grass near homes. Beautiful green surrounded her. When they entered the heart of the city, the sounds of voices and the friendly light of clay lamps burning in the houses warmed her. For the first time, she imagined what a real home with

Aden and Hashem might look like. A home with four walls and a courtyard and an oven and a table to eat at, a bedroom to sleep in, a roof to visit on hot nights.

Johanan led them to the largest home at the end of the main street. Torches lit the entrance. Cones of incense burned around the perimeter of the courtyard to keep the mosquitoes away.

Johanan announced them to Gedaliah's royal guard, who slipped into the house. A moment later, Gedaliah appeared in the courtyard, enveloping Aden in a hearty hug. "Aden ben Baruch! What a joyful and unexpected reunion this is." He turned to his servants, instructing them to prepare additional food. Odelia's tastebuds sang at the prospect.

Gedaliah stepped back, holding Aden at arm's length. "I am glad you are safe. We will speak about sensitive matters in private after we eat. But for now, come in and refresh yourselves." He turned to the soldier who had guided them. "You will join us as well, of course, Johanan. But first, please summon Baruch and Jeremiah. They will be filled with joy to see this young man."

Aden beamed, his face almost glowing beneath the warmth of the clay lamps. He ushered Odelia forward. "My lord, please allow me to introduce my wife, Odelia."

Gedaliah squinted at her. "Odelia bat Pashhur."

She straightened her spine, refusing but still managing to be cowed by the mention of her abba. "Yes."

"My grandfather had great affection for you. Welcome to my home, Daughter. It brings me joy to see two faithful servants of Adonai enter the covenant of marriage together."

She blinked back tears, both for the gracious welcome and how he spoke of Shaphan. "Shaphan...he is gone?"

Gedaliah's wizened face did not disguise his sorrow. "He passed away in his sleep hours before the Babylonians broke through the Middle Gate. May he rest with his ancestors."

Aden squeezed her hand. Of course, coming here would give them news they had only been able to assume. Did Gedaliah know the fate of her abba? Would he fault her for caring for his enemy?

They entered the house, touching their lips before bringing them to Gedaliah's mezuzah. What a blessing the simple act of entering a home and acknowledging Adonai's Law was after all this time!

The servants rushed to them, slipping off the guests' sandals and washing their dusty feet in a bowl of warm water. As the young girl dried Odelia's feet with a soft linen cloth, she swallowed back a lump in her throat.

"Thank you," she whispered as the girl disappeared into the courtyard.

Flasks of watered wine were thrust in their hands, and Gedaliah led them to a sitting room with plentiful cushioned chairs and a long oak table set with decorative oil lamps. No sooner had they sat when a commotion began in the front room.

"My son! Where is he? Where is my son?"

A lean body clad in a well-worn robe and sash and with a head threaded with silver appeared in Gedaliah's room. Aden rose, and the two men embraced in an emotional exchange that swallowed up the room. Odelia choked back tears. What a beautiful welcome from abba to son. Though there was no hope for a reunion between her and her abba, she tried to imagine one such as this. She couldn't.

Well, enough. She belonged with Aden now. His family was her family.

After many moments of soft words and embracing, Aden turned to Odelia. "Abba, I'd like to introduce my wife, Odelia."

Baruch looked at Odelia and then, with huge eyes, back to his son. He made an unintelligible noise that sounded partly of surprise, partly of joy. "My son, you have a wife! A lovely wife at that." He held out his hand to take Odelia's. "Daughter, it is a great pleasure to meet you."

She bowed low to the ground. "My lord."

He lifted her up. "I am glad Adonai has seen fit to bring us together."

"As am I. Your son has been a great comfort to many over these last weeks."

Baruch clapped his hands. "There is so much to speak of. Oh!" He turned to a rail-thin man clad in a simple brown tunic who sat on a wooden bench against Gedaliah's wall. Soulful, deep eyes found hers and he dipped his head. Baruch splayed a hand toward the man. "My friend Jeremiah ben Hilkiah."

Aden stepped forward, bowing low. "My lord."

Jeremiah placed a hand on Aden's shoulder, and Odelia's husband rose, gesturing her to his side. With quaking knees, Odelia fell at the prophet's feet, bowing until her forehead touched the cool tiles of Gedaliah's floor, her covered head brushing the hem of Jeremiah's rough hair cloak. "My lord," she choked out, but her emotion and horrid tears took up the space where words should have been. He touched her shoulder, but she could not bring herself to rise, for her tears wet his feet, and the shame of her display soaked through to her core.

"Daughter."

The one gentle word did not condemn. Did he know who she was? Slowly, she lifted her head to meet his dark brown gaze. His skin sagged, dark circles beneath his eyes made him look as if he had not slept in days. He looked older than his years, the heavy responsibility laid upon his shoulders showing on his face. Still, he looked at her with interest and care now, his head slightly cocked to the side, questioning her silently in the quiet of the room.

"I am Odelia bat Pashhur."

Understanding lit his eyes.

He reached for her hand to help her stand. A slight twinkle simmered in those fathomless eyes. "As I understand it, that was your old name, yes? You are now Odelia, wife of Aden, son of Baruch. Daughter of Yahweh."

His words caused more tears to fall upon her cheeks. She swiped them away with the back of her hand. "Forgive me for my identity, and for my tears." She looked around, conscious of the horrible impression she had made on her father-in-law and their host, governor of all the land.

A small smile inched beneath Jeremiah's beard. "Do not apologize for your blood. As for your emotion... I am acquainted with tears myself."

Somber, bittersweet smiles traveled through the room, as they were all well acquainted with Jeremiah's scrolls—the grief he expressed for his people along with the dismal message he'd been commissioned to deliver.

"Please, I know there is much to discuss but first, let us eat and celebrate this reunion. We must thank Adonai for each joy He brings our way," Jeremiah said.

Gedaliah's wife and three children joined them along with Johanan and his brother, Jonathan, and a surly man called Ishmael, son of Nethaniah, who didn't seem happy to be sharing their table.

Plates of dates and figs, cucumbers, olives, grapes, and melon were set before them. Warm flatbread with coriander relish. Then came platters of meat and fish, emmer crackers, leeks and lentils, and a savory stew of lamb all cooked in the simmering juices of wild onions and garlic.

Odelia felt she might swoon with the lavishness of such a meal. Surely they would be able to bring the others, and even the ark, back here. Make homes of their own, work in the town and enjoy the company and food of these people? What would Hashem think of such a feast? Sherah would want to hear every detail upon Odelia's return, and she tried to commit each bite to memory.

Over the course of dinner, they learned that the Babylonians had released Jeremiah and Baruch at Ramah. Though welcomed to settle in Babylon under the king's protection, Jeremiah had chosen to return to Mizpah. To stay in his land, with his people, despite his own prophetic words that the future of God's people lay with those in exile. The Hebrews in Moab, Ammon, Edom, and all other countries had gathered at Mizpah under Gedaliah as well, as he had been given the blessing of King Nebuchadnezzar to rule over them.

"A blessing from Nebuchadnezzar." The soldier named Ishmael nearly spat on his empty plate. "The king's resistance should not have failed."

The young man's outburst caused those at the table to quiet. Aden looked from the soldier to Gedaliah. "King Zedekiah is…"

Ishmael laid a heavy hand on the table. "Gone. Forced to watch the execution of his sons before being blinded and dragged in chains to Babylon."

"Ishmael." Gedaliah's sharp voice cut across the table to where the soldier hunched over his untouched food. "We are at the table, and in the presence of the women. Save your disgruntled talk for later."

Ishmael pushed his chair back and stood, forcing a bow to those at the table before storming off.

Gedaliah cleared his throat as the servants began taking away their plates and refreshing their wine. "Please excuse him. He has taken the king's demise hard." He sighed. "He is also unhappy that King Nebuchadnezzar has placed me in charge of our people. To some, my urging to follow Jeremiah's advice and submit to the Babylonians looks like weakness." Gedaliah looked around at the bowls of quince compote and platters of sweet cakes filled with pistachios and honey that the servants set before them. "But we will talk more after we enjoy our desserts, hmm?"

They dug into the sweet treats, Odelia stifling a moan of pleasure at the burst of flavors dancing on her tongue. She eyed the platter, wondering if she might ask the servant girl to pack some cakes for her and Aden to take back to Secacah for the others.

While talk surrounding the table turned lighter, Odelia saw Jeremiah staring at Ishmael's empty plate, a pensive look on his face. She thought of the young man's anger. Did the prophet know something about Ishmael the rest of them did not?

CHAPTER TWENTY-TWO

After dinner, most of the men departed to attend to their families and posts. Gedaliah's wife and children bid their guests good night and the servants brought in skins of barley beer and serving cups with straws so they could avoid the casings floating to the top.

Odelia shook her head when the servant girl who'd washed her feet earlier came to her. "I fear I have had enough wine. Perhaps some water or tea?"

The girl nodded.

"Tirza can take you to our guest room, Odelia, if you are tired?" Gedaliah said.

A wave of disappointment washed over her at his obvious suggestion that she leave them. She had wanted to spend more time with her father-in-law and Jeremiah. She wanted to hear what the men would say.

Pushing aside her wants, she smiled at Gedaliah and rose to follow the servant girl. She should be grateful not to have to worry over the men's ponderings. She would enjoy whatever fine feather bed awaited her in Gedaliah's home and rest her travel-weary body.

But then her husband spoke, directing his words to the group, which now included Gedaliah, Jeremiah, his abba Baruch, and the brothers Johanan and Jonathan. "If it pleases each of you, I would appreciate my wife's presence. Many trials have overcome us these past weeks, as I am sure is true for you. I have appreciated my wife's counsel and wisdom."

Aden's abba raised a bushy gray brow, but Aden did not seem cowed. "All of our priests except for Eliashib and half of our soldiers were killed by the raiding Babylonian party that tracked down King Zedekiah. I will not go into details, but it was tragic for our small community."

Gedaliah's brow furrowed in obvious displeasure, but Aden continued. "I have led as best I know how with Eliashib and the other soldiers, but often Odelia has been my confidante. I know it is unorthodox, but in surprising times, I believe God uses surprising people. I cannot help but think of Deborah leading our people against Jabin and finding the favor and victory of Yahweh."

Odelia's face heated. She could not be compared to Deborah, that much was certain, but that her husband spoke his mind with this crowd—with his own abba and the famed prophet—made her fall in love with him all over again.

"Very well. She may stay if it pleases Jeremiah." Gedaliah lifted his flask to take a sip of his beer.

The prophet met her gaze. "Adonai sees the heart." He nodded at her, as if those words alone were sufficient to warrant her presence. "And I insist these two stay with me and Baruch, as our guests and family."

Warmth fell over her. She wanted to proclaim her failure, how she felt the terrible burden of the price paid for her by Yahweh, first in the sacrifices given at the temple, and then those given outside the cave at Secacah on her behalf.

Baruch cleared his throat. "Tell us, my son, of your journey. Of the ark of testimony and the treasures, of what happened to the priests."

Aden told their account—from their tunnel travels with the ark, to their journey to the Salt Sea, to the rebuilding of the tabernacle and hiding it in a cave, to the terrible night of the attack, to the difficult decisions made after, including appointing Aden as high priest.

When he finished, the room grew silent, grief giving way to awkwardness as they realized the weightiness of Aden's words.

"You have been making the sacrifices and entering the Holy Place?"

Aden wet his lips. "I have not been behind the curtain of the ark, in what we constructed as the Most Holy Place, since we set it up in the Kohlit cave. But yes, in all other regards, I have been acting as high priest to intercede for our people."

"You are not of the Levitical line." Johanan sat back in his chair, brow furrowed.

Gedaliah wore a similar expression.

Finally, Baruch spoke. "Though I think of Aden as my son in the truest sense of the word, he is not of my blood."

"I do not understand." Gedaliah leaned on the oak table.

"He was orphaned and left with Shaphan as a babe. My wife and I took him in not long after we lost our own child. His blood father was of the Levitical line."

"It is unorthodox to have a priest who did not grow up in a Levitical family to serve in the temple," Gedaliah said. "I should think my grandfather would have mentioned this information to me at some point."

She opened her mouth then closed it. But no, she must speak on behalf of her husband. "If you please." Her voice started shaky but grew in strength as she realized she'd already begun something she must finish. "My husband was hesitant to take the position. He agreed to it only because He believed it to be the will of Yahweh, as did Eliashib." She turned to Jeremiah. "My lord, you wrote in your scrolls of the lies and idolatry of the priests who served in the temple in Jerusalem. Priests raised in Levitical families. My husband is seeking the ways of Yahweh. Surely, in Adonai's eyes, that is more important than how one was raised in such times of extreme trial?"

She waited, the room's silence engulfing her. Had she said too much? As a woman, anything might be too much in this room. Yet how could she stand by and allow them to think Aden did something unworthy, or worse, that he sought a high position for himself out of greed when he'd been so reluctant to take the position in the first place?

Jeremiah nodded. "I cannot say the woman is wrong. And though it is too soon, perhaps this is the beginning of what Yahweh declared when he said the ark would no longer be remembered."

Aden cleared his throat and turned to the prophet. "That brings us to another question, my lord. I am still in possession of the earthenware jar containing the deed of land you bought from your kinsman, as well as a copy of your complete scrolls, which we read to the people at Secacah."

Jeremiah nodded encouragement for Aden to continue.

Aden swallowed. "I wondered if the exiles in Babylon possess a copy of the latter part of the scrolls, the scrolls that speak of Yahweh's future promises. It is something that troubled me in Secacah as I pondered what may have happened to you and my abba."

Jeremiah's face softened. "Your heart is for your people, Aden ben Baruch. Adonai is pleased by that."

The prophet's words to her husband were like a sweet anointing of oil over the room.

Aden cleared his throat. "I pray it is so, my lord."

Jeremiah sighed, ran his fingers over the edge of his clay plate. "Yahweh will raise up other prophets in Babylon to minister to the people. I am certain of this. And remember, a few years ago I sent the scroll with Seraiah to be read to the exiles in Babylon. After he read it, he threw it into the Euphrates to symbolize the eventual sinking of Babylon."

Odelia's breath caught. She had not realized this. "Then the exiles know of the new covenant."

"I pray they have kept it close to their hearts. Nevertheless, I am uncertain if the words were copied. With more of our people going to Babylon, it would be wise for them to possess the words of hope Adonai has given me, and perhaps the words of lament I have been meditating on."

Words of lament? Were these new scrolls?

Jeremiah continued. "Your abba and I plan to travel to Babylon soon. I have been recovering at Mizpah under Gedaliah, and once my strength is returned, we plan to seek an audience with King Nebuchadnezzar."

Aden released an audible breath. "This is good news. These words have sustained not only me and my wife these last weeks but our entire community. They have given us hope for the future of our people. By now, those in exile have certainly understood the seriousness of your warnings. I pray they are remembering Adonai in their trials. I am trusting that your scroll will help sustain them."

Jeremiah turned to Baruch. "Your son not only has the bloodline of a priest, he has the heart of one."

Baruch nodded, his eyes shining as he looked at Aden. "His imma, also born of the Levites, would be proud."

They spoke more, reporting details of the destruction of Jerusalem. If Odelia imagined the night of the attack as the worst of her life, she was forced to relive the account again and again as Gedaliah and Johanan reported the atrocities committed against their people and the temple.

Baruch rubbed his forehead. "Whether or not the ark will be remembered in the future, I am convinced it honored Adonai to remove it before it could be desecrated by the invading army."

Odelia squeezed Aden's hand, asking a wordless question.

"Have you news of Odelia's family? Her parents or kinsmen?"

Gedaliah's mouth drew into a tight frown. "Your family was taken with the others into Babylon. I have not yet heard anything regarding their fate."

Odelia pressed her lips together, her gaze lifting to Jeremiah's. The prophet seemed to understand her thoughts, for he shifted in his seat. "You are thinking my prophecy was wrong or that Adonai will curse you for not following your family into Babylon."

She nodded. "When you gave my abba the name *Magor-Missabib*, you also prophesied that his family would go into exile. I assumed that meant all his family."

"There are sixty years left of the exile, Daughter. The word of Yahweh has not yet been wrong."

A chill chased up her spine. What did he mean? Would the Babylonians come again and take their remnant, including her, to Babylon? She thought of Hashem's question to Aden after he'd read Jeremiah's scrolls. If those in Babylon were to be the future hope of Judah, should she not wish to hasten there?

But the thought of going to the people who had destroyed and desecrated her city, of going to the people of the soldier who had attacked her that horrible night, filled her with dread. Perhaps, if she had a chance to speak with Jeremiah later, she would ask him for clarity. Perhaps the group who had rescued the ark would be exempt. Or perhaps she was no longer considered Pashhur's family since she married Aden.

Johanan tapped his fingers on the table and turned to Gedaliah. "We should discuss Ishmael, my lord."

Gedaliah inhaled a deep breath, releasing it slowly. "My commander here is worried about our friend Ishmael. As you may have been able to surmise at dinner, he is an angry young man, bitter over the fact that someone he sees as a traitor to King Zedekiah was placed in charge as governor."

Johanan straightened. "You have assured him multiple times you are on the side of our people in relation to the Babylonians, not a Babylonian imposed upon us. I do not see what more evidence he needs. You are Shaphan's grandson. You have encouraged the return of fruit in the land, of good work and a bountiful harvest."

Gedaliah's face reddened, as he was obviously uncomfortable with the praise.

But Jeremiah nodded. "You protected me from lynching. During the reign of King Jehoiakim, you had hopes that the publication of my scroll might change government policy and cause our people to surrender to King Nebuchadnezzar."

Gedaliah spewed out a humorous laugh. "A lot of good that did us. I am still haunted by nightmares of King Jehoiakim burning that precious scroll, slice by slice."

"You are haunted by it?" Baruch gave Gedaliah an incredulous look. "It is I who had to reconstruct my painstaking work."

"And you did it without complaint, my friend." Jeremiah smiled. "What King Jehoiakim did was an abomination of the highest order, but we commit ourselves to Yahweh and keep our gaze on Him."

Gedaliah turned to Aden. "Ishmael is resentful that such a critic of the king's policies now rules over him and that we are forced to serve the Babylonians."

"My lord, I fear you do not take Ishmael seriously enough." Johanan exchanged a glance with his brother. "We have noticed him talking with his men—other bitter young men like him. There are rumors of rebellion, rumors that he has ingratiated himself with Baalis, king of the Ammonites, rumors even that Baalis has sent Ishmael to take your life."

Gedaliah tapped his fingers on the table. "While I believe Ishmael is disgruntled, I do not believe those rumors represent even a sliver of truth. All we can do is to keep vigilant. If I were to rally my commanders against Ishmael, it would not imbue any affectionate feelings between us. I will have to trust that in time, Ishmael and his comrades will see reason. Jeremiah, if you have insight into this, please speak your mind."

"You know I have never been bashful to speak my mind, but on this, Yahweh has told me nothing. I am sorry, my brother."

Gedaliah nodded. "Then we will move forward as is. In the meantime, what of our friends at Secacah?"

Odelia didn't miss Johanan and Jonathan exchanging glances, their faces growing red at the subject of Ishmael being dismissed.

Aden didn't seem to notice as he hastened to answer Gedaliah's question. "We are anxious for direction. Should we plan to bring our group back to Mizpah so we may gather with our people? Perhaps the priests here can travel with us to the tabernacle and offer the proper sacrifices before transporting the ark back here?"

Gedaliah studied Aden. Baruch bit his lip. Jeremiah stroked his beard, his pastry only half eaten on his plate.

Finally, Jeremiah spoke. "We must pray about this. Bringing the ark back too soon may not yet honor Adonai. There are still many Babylonians about." He glanced at Johanan. "Not to mention the discontent of some of the men."

"Perhaps you should return to Secacah with my son and his wife, my lord. You have not acted in your priestly role for some time, but it is fitting you be with the ark of the covenant. And it is fitting I reunite with the family I have," Baruch said.

Odelia's stomach sank. She couldn't deny she found herself eager to bring their small community to Mizpah, to live more normally among others under a governor. To live without fear. And yet to have Jeremiah and Baruch with them would be an immense blessing if they must return.

Jeremiah stared at the platter of pastries in front of him on the table. Sticky honey oozed from their seams, and if it wouldn't be looked upon so poorly, she would take another to enjoy. Jeremiah rubbed his face. "You do not listen. The ark will not be remembered."

"But does that mean we purposefully abandon it?"

"I do not yet know." Jeremiah's gaze landed on Odelia then. "Can you stay two more nights? We will pray tonight and for the next three days. I will fast and seek Adonai's will on this. Perhaps, by then, we will have an answer."

Aden glanced at Odelia, and she nodded. "We will stay."

And while it wouldn't be much of a sacrifice to sleep in a warm, soft bed, she vowed also to pray for an answer. Jeremiah seemed certain that Adonai would hear them even though they were miles from the ark, a fact that warmed Odelia's bones.

That night, as she lay in a raised bed blanketed in lamb's wool covers alongside her husband, she sighed with contentment. The earthenware jar with the deed to Jeremiah's land and the copy of his scroll was tucked at their feet, and Aden recited the words from the scroll aloud.

"'I will put my law in their minds and write it on their hearts. I will be their God, and they will be my people. No longer will they teach their neighbor, or say to one another, "Know the Lord," because they will all know me, from the least of them to the greatest.'"

She snuggled against the muscled arm of her husband, sinking into the words and promises of Yahweh instead of focusing on the potential troubles in her future. There was a new covenant coming. And if she did not live to see it, perhaps if Adonai blessed them with children of their own one day, *they* would live to see it.

That much gave her hope.

CHAPTER TWENTY-THREE

The next day, Aden and Odelia stayed in the house of Jeremiah, visiting, praying, and fasting. Though no answer came to Odelia, praying with the prophet and her husband's family encouraged her. Surely at least Jeremiah would hear from Yahweh by the time they were to leave.

But when they rose the following morning and packed the saddlebags on their mount, the earthenware jar and leather cylinder safely tucked inside, Jeremiah had yet to give them an answer. The only thing of value he'd bestowed on them was a new scroll, a poem of lament, which Aden had tucked into the jar alongside the other scroll, and the deed.

"Should we wait, Abba?" Aden asked Baruch as they conducted a few final preparations in Jeremiah's simple courtyard.

Baruch's gaze flickered in the direction of Gedaliah's home. "We expected Gedaliah to summon us this morning, but he has been quiet."

"Where is Jeremiah?" Odelia asked, more comfortable with her kind father-in-law after spending the last two days with him.

"I think I saw him going for a walk to pray. It is not uncommon."

"We will wait to bid Jeremiah farewell." Aden gave her an apologetic smile. "Although I had hoped to make it back to Secacah early tomorrow to prepare for Shabbat, I am sure the others are doing what must be done."

Odelia nodded. As much as she'd found respite in Mizpah, she missed Hashem and Eliana and Sherah. She could hardly wait to give them the pastries tucked inside her bag that Gedaliah's wife had insisted she take.

Without warning, a cry rose from the north, from the direction of the town cistern. A frantic woman came running up the dirt road, her robe twisting at her ankles, her headscarf flapping behind her. "They have taken the king's daughters! They have killed Gedaliah!"

Odelia's heart shuddered.

Baruch reached out a hand to steady the woman. "Daughter, slow down. Tell me what you saw."

Her gaze flew to Baruch and then to Odelia. "Ishmael son of Nethaniah. He and his men have killed Gedaliah! Also, they killed the Babylonian soldiers and the men of Judah who were with the governor. He threw them in the cistern and took the rest of the captives to the Ammonites. Adonai, save us!"

She flew off again, presumably to her house. Odelia gripped Aden's arm. He brought her to him, lifting her effortlessly onto the waiting chestnut. "What—what are you doing?" Terror climbed her insides. Would they leave Aden's abba and Jeremiah?

"You must ride out of town and stay hidden until we can be sure what is happening." Aden gazed at her with certainty, but while she respected and honored her husband, this was one order she did not plan to obey.

"I am not leaving you without a horse."

She spotted Jeremiah running up the road, and they hurried to meet him.

"Is it true?" Baruch asked. "Is Gedaliah dead?"

Jeremiah's bottom lip trembled. "Yes, it is true."

Aden raked a hand through his hair. "We should have listened to Johanan. Is there news of him?"

"I do not know. All I know is…many are dead. The cistern…" He shook his head. "We will not be able to stay in the land. Not anymore." Jeremiah's gaze found Aden's then Odelia's. "You have the scroll?"

Aden nodded, patting the saddlebag just behind Odelia's leg.

Jeremiah straightened. "You must take it to Babylon. Pashhur's daughter will go there after all."

Odelia's breaths quickened, and her limbs grew weak. Babylon? Yes, she and Aden had spoken of it, but that was sometime in the future. Besides, Jeremiah said he had planned to go.

"Are you sure, Jeremiah?" Baruch spoke, his eyes traveling up the road. "Surely you should accompany them."

Yes, her father-in-law spoke wisdom.

Jeremiah's dark eyes grew somber. "It is not meant to be, Brother."

The sound of hoofbeats came toward them, hard and fast, dust billowing up in the road.

"What of the ark?" Aden's voice turned desperate as he mounted behind Odelia, his body a small bit of comfort alongside her flailing strength.

Jeremiah placed his hand on the saddlebag where the earthenware jar lay. "This represents the new covenant now. The symbol of the ark is fading, but Yahweh's new hope will remain. Take the scroll to the exiles in Babylon, Aden ben Baruch and Odelia bat Adonai. Hasten, and Yahweh be with you!"

Aden turned the stallion in the opposite direction of the soldiers now bearing down upon them, Ishmael in front, astride his own mount, his body rigid and determined.

She felt her husband's hesitation. The decision to leave his abba and the prophet to Ishmael would surely stay with him forever.

"Please, come with us," Aden begged, though how they would all escape, she hadn't a clue.

"Go, my son. Find Seraiah when you reach Babylon. Be at peace." Baruch slapped the rump of the chestnut stallion, and it bolted off, leaving the two older men behind. Odelia crouched low and clung to the horse's mane, wind whipping in her face as she gripped for dear life, Aden hunched behind her, his chest against her back.

They couldn't have traveled more than the blink of an eye when the force of something she couldn't discern caused Aden to slump against her, his weight heavy behind her.

"Aden!" she screamed.

He sagged against her and released the reins. She grabbed for them with one hand while reaching for her husband with the other, her thighs squeezing the horseflesh beneath her to remain upright. But her strength failed. Aden rolled off the horse, his mantle ripped from her grasping fingers.

She screamed. The stallion reared. She resisted the urge to pull on the reins, and once the horse landed on the ground, she urged it back to where Aden lay, a soldier's arrow poking through his chest.

"Aden!" Three soldiers on horseback barreled toward them from behind.

"Odelia, go!" Aden spoke more firmly than he ever had to her, a spot of blood pooling near his armpit. "We do not have time. You must go. Beloved, I beg of you—listen to me!"

Her limbs quaked. The soldiers came closer, closer still. She slid off the stallion and reached for her husband. He grasped her hand and squeezed. "Look at me." But there was no time.

With all her strength, she pulled at him. "Get up!"

But he would not cooperate. "Odelia, look at me."

Finally, she met his eyes. "It is useless. I will only slow us down and we will both be caught. Go, ahuvati. You can still escape. Our people need you to be strong."

Strong? How could she be strong without him? She glanced at the soldiers bearing down upon them, and she knew. She could never help Aden back onto the stallion in time, and even if she did, the soldiers would catch them in an instant.

"It is well, Odelia. I love you. You *must* do this. Jeremiah knew. Go, beloved. Find my uncle in Babylon. Adonai will go with you."

Sobs took over her body, shaking her. She reached for him one more time, pressed her lips to his, but all too soon he was pushing her away and keeling back onto the ground. She couldn't leave him. They would suffer whatever fate awaited them together. Certainly, more torture awaited him if she was also left behind. But how could she leave him?

It was only the thought of Jeremiah's scroll, of her people needing the hope contained within, that allowed her to leap onto the stallion with a strength she didn't know she possessed.

In the most painful decision of her life, she turned the mount away from her beloved. "I love you, Aden. I love you!"

She did not look back, too much a coward to see what fate awaited her husband. Instead, she kicked her heels into the stallion's sides as she'd seen soldiers do on multiple occasions. She rode until she looked back and could no longer see anyone. She didn't know where she was going, only that she must escape Ishmael's men if Jeremiah's message had any chance of reaching her people.

Only, she was without her husband. Without anyone.

And now, she must find her way into the territory of her enemy.

CHAPTER TWENTY-FOUR

Odelia ran her mount as hard as she could for what seemed like hours, her mind numb to the jostling of the stallion, to the hot sun beating upon her. She didn't know where she was, didn't know how she would get to Babylon from here. In the darkest of moments when immense waves of grief threatened to overtake her, she hardly cared.

She passed an abandoned village, and soon after, the stallion slowed at a grove of trees with a trickling river. She looked behind her. Still no sign of Ishmael's men. More than likely, they gave up on her—and her horse—long ago.

Beside the river, she slid off the animal's back. She leaned her head against its damp, smooth coat and finally allowed the whole of her grief to consume her.

Deep, retching sobs worked through her body, overshadowing her, and she fell to the ground alongside the river, face down, her tears mixed with the wailing and groanings of grief. She poured the sand of the river onto her head and thought of Aden with an arrow piercing his beautiful body. Had they killed him immediately? She prayed they hadn't tortured him. Or had they thrown him in the cistern with his comrades to die a slow death?

She imagined him with his abba and Jeremiah, suffering among the dead and dying. Fresh anguish consumed her. They should have listened to Johanan. Or perhaps they should have never come to Mizpah at all.

Her friends at Secacah would be waiting for them. And Hashem. Would the boy think they abandoned him? How much could one child endure and not be hardened by the horrors of life?

For a moment, she thought about disregarding Jeremiah and Aden's commands and returning to Secacah. Perhaps Jehoahaz or even Hashem could help her to Babylon. She could rest before her travels, assure Hashem, seek comfort in the arms of Sherah and Eliana.

After she'd spent all her tears, she lay face down in the dirt, listening to the trickle of the river. "Adonai…" she began. While part of her wanted to rail against the God of her people, a stronger part desired to run to Him. In this moment, He was all she had left.

"I am poor in spirit, Adonai. I am sodden with grief. Answer me!"

Another wave of tears coursed down her cheeks, but she heard nothing aside from the steady flow of the river. Familiar doubt niggled its way into the deepest parts of her. She inched on her belly toward the water and drank from its coolness, splashed its lifegiving moisture onto her face.

She thought of the earthenware jar in the saddlebag, the deed to the land at Anathoth, two scrolls she likely could not read. Aden had placed all his hope in these things—but not the way her people had placed hope in the temple instead of Yahweh. Her husband's hope in these items lay in what they represented.

She could not disappoint him.

With much effort, she pushed herself to her feet and untied the saddlebag before fishing out some figs and nuts. She forced them into her mouth, though her stomach rebelled. She fed the stallion emmer crackers before pulling out the map Jehoahaz had given them and finding the spot Aden had shown her marking Mizpah. She knew Babylon lay to the northeast, but what if she ran into Ishmael's gang or the Ammonites? What if she could not find the empire she sought?

She peered at the sun, already beginning its descent, and vowed to start out again the next day. Both she and the horse needed rest. There was something about this place that spoke of safety, and if she rode now, she may not find another spot to sleep.

Taking out some blankets, she then tied the horse to a nearby tree and found a soft patch of grass to lie down in. Against her better judgment, she took out the new scroll Jeremiah had given Aden that morning and struggled to make out the words. It was slow going, and the scroll held no such promises of hope, but it mirrored her heart. She wept as she read what she could, owning every sorrow-drenched word for herself.

No one is near to comfort me, no one to restore my spirit....
The Lord has rejected his altar and abandoned his sanctuary...

And then she came to a line that felt like breathing air after a time of drowning.

My soul is downcast within me.
Yet this I call to mind
and therefore I have hope:
Because of the Lord's great love, we are not consumed,

for his compassions never fail.
They are new every morning;
great is your faithfulness.

Spent from grief, she clung to that last promise, allowing the sweet darkness of sleep to overtake her.

"Odelia."

The voice came around her and on top of her all at once, causing her to jolt upright in her sleep.

Had she been dreaming?

She opened her eyes and blinked. A man in a bright white robe stood before her. Though she ought to be frightened, she wasn't.

"Who are you?"

"I am your strength."

Her mouth grew dry. She could not take her eyes off the gleaming white of the robe, so pure and shining, the brightest priestly robe she'd ever known. Was this an angel, perhaps, like the one Jacob saw in his dream? But no, she knew with robes that white, this man was a priest of the highest order. A priest of heaven? Why was he here?

"Adonai?"

"I am the Lord, compassionate and gracious, slow to anger, abounding in love and faithfulness. Daughter, do not be afraid to do as Jeremiah instructed."

She wept, overwhelmed by the fullness of His love. She had not been forgotten after all. Despite everything, He loved her.

"Yahweh, be with me."

"Do not fear, for I am with you; do not be dismayed, for I am your God. I will strengthen you and help you. I will uphold you with my righteous right hand. This is my covenant."

"May it be as You say, Adonai." Odelia bowed her face to the ground.

When she woke, dawn brightened the grove of trees. The stallion pawed the ground, anxious to be moving.

Odelia sat up and blinked. It hadn't been a dream, had it? Why would Adonai come to her, and in the form of a man? He quoted Moses's words to her, and Isaiah's. Had her grief-stricken brain conjured the image?

But no. She knew the truth of the angel's words, telling her not to fear. She was not alone.

She nodded, as if to solidify the truth within her soul once more before mounting the stallion and urging him out of the safety of the grove of trees.

She did not understand the tragic events that had befallen her. But she knew with certainty that Adonai was with her.

And He would be with her no matter if she ran into Ishmael's crew or stumbled upon a fierce group of Babylonians and faced death at their hand.

"I am Your servant, Yahweh," she whispered, strength coursing to her limbs.

She aimed her mount north and dug her heels into the chestnut's sides.

When she spotted the Babylonian soldiers with their pointed helmets on the highway two days later, she directed the chestnut behind the ragged brush off the road, ducking low to press herself into the horseflesh, praying for them to pass without spotting the gleaming flanks of her horse.

The stallion pawed the ground at the approach of the other horses, and Odelia shrank into herself, squeezing her eyes shut.

"Show yourself!" a harsh voice called in Aramaic.

She straightened and threw her shoulders back as she nudged the chestnut with her heels, reins tight in her hands.

The first soldier stood high on his mount as he approached her, an amused smile tipping his lips. "What have we here? It seems Marduk has sent a little Jewess to keep us company."

A Jewess? She had never heard the term. Chills chased up and down her arms as she remembered the soldier attempting to drag her out of the tent. Should she have tried to outrun them? But her horse was tired and in need of food—they would have certainly overtaken her.

Adonai had told her not to fear. No matter if those bright and shining white robes were not visible now, He was with her.

Another soldier came around to her side, eyeing her. "She would make good travel company."

"That is enough." Another man, with an oiled beard and gleaming white teeth, came up behind them. Though shorter in stature, he appeared to command the rest, and for that reason, Odelia's stomach unclenched. She still did not know where she was going—the reality was that this contingent was her best hope in taking her to Aden's uncle Seraiah.

She dipped her head. "My lord."

"You are a long way from your people." His broken Hebrew was not smooth, but at least he spoke it to her, as opposed to the more common Aramaic the Babylonians tended to use.

"I come from Mizpah, where Gedaliah the governor and the prophet Jeremiah resided. I was there when Ishmael, son of Nethaniah, killed the governor and my husband. I am on my way to Babylon to see my husband's uncle, Seraiah."

She held her breath. Surely Seraiah would remember her. If not, he would recognize Aden's seal. Seraiah would be well regarded in Babylon, as one who had urged King Zedekiah to surrender to the Babylonians.

The soldier with the oiled beard eyed her. "I know Seraiah. We are on our way to the city now. We will see that you arrive there safely." He glared at his subordinates. "And if anyone should lay a hand on this Jewess, let them know they will have me to deal with."

She dipped her head again, the prick of tears coming to the backs of her eyelids. "Thank you, my lord."

She stayed with the soldiers for twenty-five days. After the first night, when she shared the honeyed pistachio pastries, they began to treat her with a distant, sisterly comradery. They gave her first choice of the woods to take care of her needs, and occasionally, the leader of the group, whose name was Tiamet, would insist she ride in the front with him. And although she took many occasions to study each man, wondering if any happened to be the soldier in her tent that terrible night, she could not come to any conclusions.

The memories that haunted her were not the only reason she refused their tents. The sight of the metal statues they placed outside their abodes caused her to keep far away when they made camp. Tiamet told her the idol's name was Sirrush, a fanciful creature of many animal parts that represented the Babylonian patron god, Marduk.

Her grief numbed with the odd sense that came with her circumstances. She found it easier to think of Aden as alive somewhere in Mizpah, waiting for her to return. And even if it were not true, the denial was one she willingly sank into, as it put fresh fervor behind her mission.

She would do it for the glory of Yahweh, yes, but she would also do it for Aden. Once she found Seraiah, all would be well. He would help her get back to Hashem and the others. Her chest ached at the thought of living in Secacah without Aden. What she would give to live a lifetime in the simple tents and caves of Secacah if it meant having her husband by her side!

The morning of their twenty-fifth day found them at the gates of Sippar, the Babylonian trading city situated at the place where the Euphrates River split into several branches. From there, they boarded a large round boat called a *kuphar*.

Lush vegetation alongside reed houses ushered them down the river. It spoke of luxury and food and abundance Odelia had never known. When they reached the plain of Dura, she glimpsed a large gold statue, at least three score cubits high. Was this the king's image? Did it serve to frighten passersby? If so, he succeeded with her. She shivered as their boat floated by the massive figure of gold.

What a strange and powerful nation to have a king who tore down cities and set up such statues on grand rivers.

Not long after, Odelia sucked in a breath at the sight of Nebuchadnezzar's city, tucked up against the River Euphrates. High walls surrounded the capital, and Tiamet proudly described the structure of the city gates, as if boasting about an intelligent son. The Urash Gate, meaning, "The Enemy is Abhorrent to It," and the Adad Gate, a plea for the god Adad to guard the troops. Tiamet spoke of another gate—the largest of all—that the king planned to build in the future.

She listened with interest as they passed through the magnificent gates etched with imaginative animals. Tiamet nodded to guards from their positions at each gate parapet. The entrances, their tops reaching to the heavens, unfolded their arms to allow them passage into the city.

They rode over a moat and abundant crops, palms and other leafy and colorful trees, and canals that spoke to a fertile, abundant land. The bustle and noise of the city and market was nothing like the City of David, nor were the beautiful villas lining the high street they traveled upon. The clothes of the city dwellers proved as colorful as a rainbow, as if all were royalty.

Odelia glimpsed a massive ziggurat temple surrounded by a wall cut with multiple gates, smoking incense at each entrance. She shivered. Statues of copper dragons guarded its entrance.

Tiamet laughed. "Does the Esagila Temple strike fear into you?" He pointed to the top of the monument, shining with jewels and fantastical images. "That is where Marduk lives, watching over our city."

Odelia nodded, trying not to question Jeremiah's words. How was the hope and future of her people here, in this city? A new ache for Solomon's Temple overwhelmed her. But it was destroyed, all while the Babylonian god flourished here in his high perch.

She bit her lip, reminded herself of her dream, the presence of the man in the white robe, the promise that came with it. If all she had for the rest of her days was that encounter, it was better than any Babylonian temple.

"I will deliver you to the Southern Palace, where your kinsman Seraiah works. Perhaps, if Marduk smiles upon you, you will be able to glimpse the Hanging Gardens at the Northern Palace someday."

"I thank you, Tiamet. You have treated me, a foreigner and a woman traveling alone, with more kindness than some of my own family. For that, I am grateful."

His face colored. "It is my duty."

He led her past more guards and more walls, into a palace grander than anything Odelia had ever seen. The royal stable hands took the chestnut and Tiamet's horse. The soldier then led her into an enormous throne room decorated with lions and fantastic trees, lapis lazuli-glazed reliefs, and brightly colored tapestries. She swallowed a fresh wave of grief as she remembered her circumstances, missing her husband anew. She had made it to their destination, but what now?

Tiamet guided her to a side room and instructed her to wait until he returned. She clutched Aden's earthenware jug and the leather cylinder, the only possessions with her, tightly to her chest. A map lay open on a polished wooden table, and she approached it, recognizing the Aramaic words but unable to read them.

"Odelia bat Pashhur."

She whirled to see a soldier. But not any soldier, for the weathered, familiar face was that of Aden's uncle. Though they did not share blood, they did share a slight resemblance in their aquiline noses, a feature so common among her people. It was enough to cause her to quell unexpected emotion as she fell at his feet. "My lord!"

He bid her to stand, laying one hand at her elbow. "Daughter, you have been through much, no doubt. The king has given me a guest room near my quarters. Come, we will get you settled, and then you can tell me of your journey."

Seraiah thanked Tiamet, and Odelia bowed farewell to her traveling companion before following Aden's uncle past a winding maze of corridors. Unfamiliar statues and drawings and high windows illuminated their way, and she became cognizant of her dirtied state. When Seraiah opened a door for her to the most lavish room Odelia had ever seen, and a servant girl began to wash her feet, the prick of tears burned the back of her eyelids.

How could she be in Nebuchadnezzar's palace? Was she not a traitor to her people to be sitting in this most luxurious room with the scent of lavender and roses meeting her nostrils while her husband and Jeremiah and Baruch had been thrown into a cistern to languish and die? And Hashem, Eliana, Sherah, and Jehoahaz left wondering about her and Aden's fate?

She must return to Secacah, to her people. She handed Seraiah Aden's jar. "It contains the deed and some of Jeremiah's scrolls. It is the hope for our people. It is why I came. Perhaps now I can return to Secacah?" How could she sleep on that fine feathered bed, on sheets perfumed with myrrh, while her friends did not know her fate, while her husband's body lay buried in a Mizpah cistern?

Seraiah glanced at the servant girl. "You may leave us."

The girl obeyed, closing the door behind her, leaving Odelia alone with Seraiah in this palace room.

"You are tired, Daughter. We have much to talk about, but you must rest first. I will have food brought to you. But please do not try to leave. You may have walked willingly through the city gates, but understand, Nebuchadnezzar's men are under strict orders not to let any Hebrews leave. I am afraid you will not be returning to Secacah."

Not returning... Of course. Why did she think they would allow her to leave? Even Aden's uncle, however privileged his position, was a prisoner.

The tears no longer held back. She wilted against Seraiah, not caring for the impropriety, not caring that she was dirty from her long journey.

She had done what she came to do, and truth be told, she would do it all over again if given the choice. For Yahweh's words were now among His people. His hope, for all to possess and look forward to. She would give up all she knew and loved for this most important of tasks.

Yahweh, great is Your faithfulness.

Adonai had seen her this far. And despite the grief wracking her body, she trusted that He would not leave her now.

CHAPTER TWENTY-FIVE

Odelia didn't know how long she slept on the soft feather mattress. When she awoke, a tray of soft cheeses and a variety of crackers lay before her alongside figs and bread with date paste. An hour after she had consumed the food, the servant girl, a young Hebrew named Aliza, brought her a bone broth with onions and garlic as well as chickpeas flavored with coriander and honey. She ate and felt her strength return, along with clear thoughts.

Aliza helped her bathe and dress in linen garments of the softest wool. She knelt on a brightly colored floor mat, facing south toward the wreckage that was Jerusalem. She prayed for a long while, the scent of burning lotus cones eliciting a foreign reassurance. She beseeched Adonai for the community at Secacah. She prayed for the captives of Ishmael's group. She prayed for her people here in Babylon. And she thanked Him for seeing the scrolls safely to her people.

When a knock came to her door, she opened it to find a Hebrew boy no older than Hashem standing in the hall.

"I am to take you to Seraiah."

She nodded, following him a few doors down to another chamber. The boy led her into a room much like her own but with a larger sitting area and walls painted with elaborate garden scenes. A table with multiple maps took up the center.

Seraiah stood in the middle of the room, tall and handsome in a regal robe instead of the garb of a soldier. He looked healthy and well-fed, his skin no longer wasting away upon his bones as it was when she first saw him that long ago day in Solomon's Temple, when Shaphan invited her to the inner rooms.

She went to him, bowing low, catching his pleasant scent of spikenard and cedar. Again, he lifted her up.

"Are you rested, Daughter?"

"Yes, thank you."

He gestured for her to sit in an ornate stuffed chair. "We have much to discuss." Once she was seated, Seraiah dismissed the boy and sat in the chair adjacent to her.

"Please, my lord. If you could first assure me that Jeremiah's scrolls are in safe hands, I would be grateful."

"They are. There is a young man here I would trust with my life who has found favor with the king. He has followed Jeremiah's instructions to serve the king, and yet he has remained faithful to Adonai. His name is Daniel. He will copy the scrolls and see to their distribution."

Jeremiah had mentioned there would be other prophets Adonai would raise up. Might this Daniel be one of them?

Pressure drained from her chest. The scrolls were no longer her responsibility. She had done what Jeremiah asked her to do. Adonai would carry out His plan regardless of her, and that fact soothed her.

"I am grateful Yahweh has seen them into this Daniel's hands. I pray our people are filled with hope by the words contained in them, as I have been. As my husband was."

"Your husband?"

"Yes, my lord. Aden ben Baruch, your nephew."

Seraiah's eyes lit. "You married. How fitting. Tell me, what has happened to my nephew?"

Slowly, and not without tears, Odelia recounted what happened at Mizpah to both Seraiah's brother, Baruch, and to Aden.

"We have known much grief in this time. My brother and his son were among the most faithful men I have had the privilege of knowing."

Odelia bit her lip. "Yes."

"Tell me how you came to Mizpah. Did you make it to Secacah? What of the ark?"

The journey poured from her mouth. She did not hold back in telling Seraiah everything—of their time in the tunnels, the near starvation that threatened to leave them dead, their travel to Secacah, and the hiding of the ark and the temple treasures. Finally, she told him of the attack and her marriage to Aden shortly after Aden's anointing ceremony, of their tragic time in Mizpah.

Aden's uncle stared at her, his mouth agape. "Daughter, so much in so little time." He grew quiet. "My Hannah died in the first deportation, more than ten years ago." He cleared his throat. "Odelia, I have always thought of Aden as my true nephew. I know it is soon, but I want you to know I am willing to take up my responsibility as your kinsman redeemer."

Her mouth grew dry. "That is not why I have come to you. I did not expect—"

"I know. But you are in a foreign city without an abba or husband. If you throw yourself at the mercy of the throne, you will be a slave or forced to work as a temple prostitute. If you are fortunate, you might find a merchant who would hire you. Do you have skills?"

"I weave baskets. I know a bit of healing."

It sounded pitiful even to her own ears. Slowly, clarity came over her. If she did not accept Seraiah's protection—the protection he had earned beneath King Nebuchadnezzar as a proponent of Jerusalem surrendering to the foreign king—she would be forced to serve the Babylonian god. To work at the Esagila in the most detestable of ways. How would she survive it?

"You have some time here, but it will not be forever. I realize marriage is not on your mind in the midst of your grief, but you must decide," Seraiah said.

"My lord, do you know of my parents' fate?"

Seraiah's lined face grew more so, and she realized he must be older even than his brother Baruch. "Your imma perished shortly after they arrived in the city. Your abba is here, imprisoned in the palace."

She pushed down the sharp sting of yet another loss. Her imma gone. And yet it was a mercy that she was not languishing alongside her abba in a prison.

"Will you take me to him?" She had not answered Seraiah's proposal, and yet surely he would understand her wanting to see her abba.

"The palace prison is not a place for a young woman. Your abba suffers ill health and circumstances, and though I have sought to improve them and those of our people, it has done little good." He gazed on the colorful painting on his wall. "You realize that those most resistant to surrender have fared the worst. It would not benefit you for anyone to find out you are Pashhur's daughter."

"Please, my lord, take me to him."

"He is not long for this world, Odelia. Perhaps it best you remember him as he was."

"We did not part well, if you remember. In fact, I ran from my home in the dark of night like a criminal."

"You did what Shaphan asked to protect the ark. You did right. Do not doubt that now."

"I do not." She spoke softly. "I only wish I could better understand Adonai's ways. What good is our bringing the ark to Secacah if it is hidden there with only a single priest to tend it? My abba views me as a traitor, and I am without my husband."

He reached for her hand, and she felt nothing more than fatherly concern. How could she accept him as her husband, especially with the still-fresh wave of mourning for Aden upon her? And yet, what choice did she have?

"I will take you to him if you are certain. I only pray you do not regret it."

Air escaped her lungs. "Thank you, my lord. You are kind."

"We will wait until tonight, when there are fewer guards and fewer questions as to why I am bringing a woman into the prison."

She dipped her head. "I am indebted to you."

Well after dinner that night, he knocked lightly on her door. She opened it, grasping at the neck of the dark wool cloak she wore. Seraiah had donned his soldier's uniform. She hated seeing him in the Babylonian dress but reminded herself it was not the outward trappings that made a man, or God. In the end, it was not the clothes or a temple or even an ark. It was the character and heart of a being that mattered.

The thought caused a fresh wave of grief to course over her at the thought of Aden and his beautiful heart. Was he with the man who had come to her in her dreams? The priest in white? Oh, may it be so.

Seraiah led her down a maze of corridors and stairs that traveled belowground to yet more tunnels. After they passed a set of guards, one who said something crude to Seraiah about Odelia's presence, the smell of unwashed bodies assaulted her nostrils. She gagged, lifting her cloak to her nose.

Moaning came to her from all sides, the metal prison bars closing in on her. Seraiah led her to a corner cell. He handed her a clay lamp. "You don't have much time. I will be only a few cubits away."

She opened her mouth to thank him but then caught sight of her abba. Her regal, priestly abba, who would never so much as deign to wash his own feet, hunched on the cement floor of the jail cell. She fell at the bars, reaching a hand toward him. "Abba!"

He glanced up at her with glazed eyes. His hair lay unkempt at his shoulders, his robe torn and thin, his ghostly face clammy in the dim light of her lamp.

"Abba, I am here."

He stared at her. "Daughter?"

She cleared her throat. "Yes, it is I, Odelia." She reached for him, and he raised his hand to her. Just as their fingers were to touch though, he snatched his hand and buried it in his mantle.

"I have no daughter."

"But I am here. I came to Babylon."

"My daughter is dead to me. She left her imma and me to save herself." His words lashed her with a cold harshness she should have expected. Still, she lurched backward.

This was the man who'd had Jeremiah whipped. The man willing to sell her to the drunkard Adino. She should not have entered the prison without remembering these truths, remembering Abba's character.

"I saw no other choice, Abba. I helped to save the ark of the covenant from the invading army. Is that not worthy in your sight? Please, Abba…"

But he did not answer.

"Tell me what you need. I will try to come again. I will bring you blankets and perhaps some food—"

"I do not wish to see you."

"Abba, you cannot mean that. I am your flesh and blood."

His gaze flicked to her for the briefest of moments, but he remained mute.

"I have learned of Adonai's future promises, Abba." She would not mention that she herself brought the words to her people captive in Babylon. She would not mention that the words came from Jeremiah. She would not say anything that would further turn him away from Adonai.

Instead, she simply spoke the words she'd long ago committed to her heart. "'The days are coming,' declares the Lord, 'when I will make a new covenant with the people of Israel and with the people of Judah.… This is the covenant I will make with the people of Israel after that time,' declares the Lord.'"

He would think her bold and impudent to be spouting words at him—words he would likely not believe. But they were all she had. "'I will put my law in their minds and write it on their hearts. I will be their God, and they will be my people. No longer will they teach their neighbor, or say to one another, 'Know the Lord,' because they will all know me, from the least of them to the greatest,' declares the Lord. 'For I will forgive their wickedness and will remember their sins no more.'"

A tear fell down her cheek. "Is that not good news, Abba? Even now, He will forgive us."

Still, he did not speak.

"It is time, Odelia." Seraiah approached the cell.

She stood. "I will return."

"Do not." Her abba's words came like ice.

"Shalom, Abba." She followed Seraiah out of the prison, a fierce determination growing inside her. Her abba may never accept Yahweh's mercy or forgiveness. He may cling to his muleheaded ways, mourn the temple he worshiped while missing the God it was built for. But nevertheless, she would return. Adonai had given her a new heart, and it was one with which the only answer to her question was love.

CHAPTER TWENTY-SIX

A week passed, and then another. Odelia's skin glowed with health after days of good food and good rest. Her head clear, her mind sharper and more alert than it had been in months.

Seraiah was patient. He came to her one morning after another visit to her abba. Though she had brought her abba blankets and food and warm herbal drinks when she could, singing the songs of Miriam and David to him, he had not warmed to her.

"Odelia, I fear the time has come. The guards have noticed your presence. They question why I allow you to continue visiting your abba. My own commanding officer has questioned your long stay in the palace. I fear he will go to Nebuzaradan, the commander of the imperial guard. I am treated well here, but my position is not one of authority."

She lowered herself to a chair in the small sitting room Seraiah had provided for her. She had many privileges here, and yet what mattered to her most was ministering to her abba, doing as Adonai commanded, and living in peace among the Babylonians.

She glanced at her bed, at the feather pillow never dry from her nightly tears. While peace and hope flooded her being, she still deeply grieved her husband. Could she share another man's bed—a man old enough to be her abba—while tears for Aden still soaked into her pillow?

And yet, could she relegate herself to a life of slavery? To serving as a temple prostitute? It was unthinkable. Seraiah was kin. He was willing to take her in. She could live in relative comfort. Perhaps continue to learn to read. She could find ways to minister to her people, here in the city.

But her heart grieved for Aden. What would he think of her wedding his uncle? And yet, deep in her heart, she knew her husband expected this, perhaps had even sent her to Seraiah hoping she would be brought beneath the umbrella of protection of his family. He would want her to agree to Seraiah's proposition.

If she wished to live and flourish and care for her abba in his remaining days, what other choice did she have?

"I accept your offer as my kinsman redeemer and to marriage, Seraiah. And I am grateful. Thank you."

He smiled, but it was a sad one born of hardship. "I pray our unification will be a blessed one and pleasing to Adonai. I will care for you, Odelia." He drew her close and placed a chaste kiss on her head. "I will see about the ceremony and a simple celebration."

When he was gone, she pressed her lips together to keep from crying. This would not be a marriage born of love and passion. This would be a different sort of marriage, and yet that did not mean it could not bring blessing on her and her people.

She dropped to her bed and once again laid her head on her pillow. As usual, her prayers mingled with her tears, her heart aching anew for Aden. For Hashem. For all those at Secacah. When she rose for dinner, she straightened her spine, reminding herself of the glimpse of heaven Adonai had given her. His words.

Do not fear.

And she didn't. Even amid her grief and sorrow, what Adonai had uprooted, one day, maybe even now, He would begin to build up once again.

"I have spoken to Nebuzaradan about your abba."

"Oh?" Hope climbed Odelia's insides as she and Seraiah broke bread for their noon meal.

"He has agreed to release your abba once we are married. He did not think it fitting a soldier of the palace to have a father-in-law in prison."

She reached out a hand to Seraiah, affection coursing through her. "My lord, that is wonderful news. Thank you."

"I am happy to please you. I have spoken to the priests, and a small ceremony will be held tomorrow."

She swallowed. "Tomorrow."

The heat of his gaze lay heavy upon her. "I know a longer time would be ideal, but considering all our people have gone through and that you are a single woman who has stayed in my guest room for weeks, we must not tarry. The guards are beginning to talk." His tone wasn't sharp, exactly, but it held an edge of impatience she hadn't yet heard from him.

"Of course, my lord. I am grateful for all you have done, for offering me so much when I have so little to give."

He reached for her hand. "What you have is enough, Odelia."

She smiled, and he leaned over tentatively, his cracked lips landing on her mouth in a kiss that she knew was harder than he intended.

Later that night, they once again made their way into the cellar to visit her abba. This time, a violent coughing sounded from the cell. When Odelia reached her abba, she thrust a warm clay cup toward him. "Abba, drink this."

With trembling hands, he took the cup. "You should not be in this place," he rasped.

It was the first time he'd spoken to her since that initial day, since he had told her not to return.

"You will leave this place soon, Abba. We will get a doctor. You will be well."

The following day, after Aliza had arranged her hair and perfumed her, Odelia was ready to commit herself to Seraiah, if for no other reason than to retrieve her abba from prison. When the knock came on her door and Aliza opened it, however, Seraiah, handsome in his finest robe, wore a worried frown.

"What is it?"

"Your abba. I have just received news he has taken a turn for the worse. Would you like to go through with our nuptials so we may see him safely out of the prison, or should we delay so you may see him once again?"

Once again. Her abba would die so soon?

If they married immediately, would she shirk the duties of her wedding night to tend to her abba? Then again, if she did not marry Seraiah now, her abba would die in a dank, dark prison cell, his last breaths that of the putrid scent of the prison.

Adonai... She lifted up a wordless prayer for wisdom. No answer met her, only a certainty that she must go to her abba.

"I must see him." It might be too late if she wed Seraiah.

Seraiah nodded. "I understand. I will see if the priest can wait." He turned to the Hebrew boy, but Odelia couldn't comprehend the words. She was already calling for Aliza to help her into the old tunic she wore to the prison.

After Seraiah had also changed into his soldier's garb, they traveled the now familiar path into the bowels of the palace prison. Her abba lay in a corner of the cell, barely breathing, barely conscious.

"He has been like this for hours," the Babylonian soldier reported.

"Please, will you let me go to him?" Odelia asked.

The soldier glanced at Seraiah, who nodded. He unlocked the cell and Odelia slipped inside, gagging at the putrid scent. She crouched beside her abba's wasted form, the heat from his fevered skin emanating from him.

She ran her cool hand over his forehead, unsure what she could do for him. Zillah's training was not enough in this moment—was any healer's?

"Abba, it is I."

He stirred.

A tear coursed down her cheek. She held many feelings for this man, and until this moment, she wasn't sure love was one of them. But love was a complicated beast.

She could not agree with her abba's choices, but she could remember a rare kind smile or the one time when she was small that he allowed her to ride on his shoulders during the New Moon festival.

And then, she knew what she must do before he left this earth. Though he did not ask it of her, she would grant him all she had to offer in hopes for his peace in Sheol.

"I forgive you, Abba."

His hand moved, the slightest of flutters in his fingers as they attempted to extend toward her.

"Daughter," he said.

But then, he was gone.

Odelia wept silent tears for the loss of a relationship she never possessed with this complicated man. Had her abba's heart softened in these last days? Had he repented of his pride? She would never know, and perhaps it was not Adonai's way that she ever did know. She had answered the call to love her abba the best she knew how, and now, she clung to his last word.

Daughter.

In it, she found hope that, perhaps, she had finally made peace with the man she'd never been able to please.

Odelia's contact with her abba after his death had rendered her unclean, and so Seraiah had arranged with the priests for a simple burial for her abba and for their wedding nuptials to be performed after she had gone through the purification rituals.

As Aliza helped her with her bath and applied henna to her nails, Odelia acknowledged the great peace that was surely Adonai's presence. She had walked in His ways and would continue to seek His face, to teach her children of His Law and compassion.

And even if she never knew the kind of love she had with Aden, it would be enough.

Aliza arranged her plaited hair beneath her simple veil. Odelia had just finished donning a no-nonsense clean woolen robe when a rapid knock came at her door. She opened it to find Seraiah's servant boy.

"My master asks you come to the throne room, my lady." The boy danced from one foot to the other.

Odelia blinked. What of the music that was to accompany the bridegroom to her chamber? What of the shout from him, that he would come to claim his bride?

But she had experienced none of the traditions when she married Aden, and she did not think she could stomach them now. But why would Seraiah call her to him in such a disreputable way? Had he decided to hoist her on the mercy of Nebuchadnezzar instead of spreading his garment over her?

She steeled her back, reciting the words the man in the white robe had told her. *Do not fear, for I am with you; do not be dismayed, for I am your God. I will strengthen you and help you. I will uphold you with My righteous right hand. This is My covenant.*

Adonai was in this place. As surely as he inhabited the ark of the covenant in Solomon's Temple, as surely as He had revealed Himself to her on her escape from Mizpah, He was with her now, communing with her in prayer, no matter what the days ahead would bring her. He had written this truth on her heart, had allowed her to see the world bathed in His presence.

She followed Seraiah's servant to the throne room where a dirty, bedraggled group of Hebrew captives stood. She blinked, recognizing their familiar forms.

"Odelia!" Throwing aside propriety, Sherah ran to her.

The two friends embraced as Odelia's mind spun. "You are here. How are you here?"

Lean arms wrapped around her waist, and Odelia burrowed her face in Hashem's dirty hair, squeezing him tight, relishing the feel of his body, knowing nothing of this earthly life would ever feel so good again as holding him in her arms.

Sobs erupted past her lips, and she closed her eyes against them. "I thought I would never see you again!"

Oh, praise Adonai for this mercy! But she had so many questions. How did they come to be here? How did they know to find her here? What of the ark?

And then Eliana and Jehoahaz were hugging her, all propriety thrown aside. Nearly forgetting herself, she turned to Seraiah to introduce them to her intended but instead found herself face-to-face with a ghost.

Her knees turned to mutton jelly, giving way beneath her at the sight of the man she loved more than any other.

"Ahuvati," he said.

Beloved.

"Aden?" Was she dreaming?

But no, he was walking toward her, his steps slower, his face paler, his frame thinner, but there was no denying her husband stood before her.

And then she was in his arms, showering kisses upon his face, trying to comprehend his presence.

But none of that mattered. He *was* here, Adonai be praised.

Under the watchful eye of Nebuzaradan, Aden told Odelia and Seraiah his story.

"I was spared from the cistern," he said, after taking a drink of watered wine. "Instead, I was taken east toward Ammon with Jeremiah and my abba, along with the rest of the captives. A physician was among them, one who cared for my wound. He told me if the arrow had been less than a handbreadth to the right, I would not have lived."

Aden squeezed her hand before continuing. "I would likely not have lived if forced to travel much longer. But Johanan and Jonathan showed up and rescued us from Ishmael."

"Praise Adonai. What is the fate of Ishmael?" Seraiah asked his nephew.

"He and his comrades escaped to Ammon. Johanan saw me to Secacah but turned surly and did not permit Jeremiah to leave. He was certain the prophet's presence would bless him and those with him." Aden lowered his gaze. "My abba chose to stay with Jeremiah. We said our last goodbyes many miles outside of Mizpah."

Last Aden knew, against Jeremiah's advice, the group planned to escape to Egypt.

Odelia mourned her father-in-law and Jeremiah, saddened that these faithful men seemed destined to live and die among a faithless people. They would go to Egypt, the very place Adonai had freed them from during the Exodus all those years earlier.

And yet, Aden *was* here! With Hashem and her dear friends.

"I recovered several days at Secacah. When I could walk, I offered the proper sacrifices to Yahweh. Our entire community prayed. I knew I would go after you to Babylon, but we were unsure if Eliashib and the others would stay.

"That night, as we prayed, there was a great earthquake. So great, the cave at the hill of Kohlit sealed shut with the temple treasures buried beneath. The ark of the covenant buried deep in the cave."

A silence fell over the group as they acknowledged the parting of the ark from their people.

"Even though we knew what Jeremiah wrote about the ark, it was difficult to fathom. And yet Adonai's words about our future hope spoke to us. We were all in agreement that, with the ark buried, it was time to turn our gaze to a new future. There was no longer a reason for us to stay at Secacah."

A tear traveled down Odelia's cheek. She would not state here in front of Seraiah how close she'd come to desecrating her marriage vows to Aden, as she assumed him dead. She did not wish to hurt Seraiah, worthy man that he was, in any way. But oh, how Adonai had given her such immense grace in this matter.

Uncaring about propriety, she buried her head in Aden's chest. The next moment, Seraiah was hugging his nephew, planning a feast for the entire group.

Their future here in Babylon remained uncertain. But Odelia could place her confidence in one fact: Adonai was with them.

And that was more than enough.

CHAPTER TWENTY-SEVEN

Anathoth, Sixty Years Later

Odelia raised her hand, shading her eyes to better see the home her sons and grandsons had built with their hands on the land Jeremiah bought from his cousin all those years ago.

"It will be a fine home." Aden lowered himself to the ground beside her, the cane he now used never far from his side.

"I knew the day would come, but I wondered if Yahweh would allow us to see it with our own eyes."

The years in Babylon had been kind to their family, even as they longed to return to the land of their forefathers. Aden found work as a scribe and teacher under Daniel. He kept up with Odelia's lessons, and she became something of an unofficial teacher herself in the ways of the Law.

She found her joy in raising their five children. Three boys, including Hashem, followed by two daughters. Her heart burst after Cyrus's decree, which stated that the temple in Jerusalem should be rebuilt, that whoever wished to return to their homeland could do so. Aden and Odelia's family had agreed to build their homes here in Anathoth upon the land that symbolized the hope of Adonai's promise. Sherah and Jehoahaz's families would arrive soon to help them begin the town.

When the family of Aden ben Baruch first arrived, Aden had dug out the deed from the earthenware jar and poured oil over it, anointing the land and dedicating it to Yahweh.

Odelia had cried happy tears, and Hashem had hugged her. "We have seen with our own eyes that Adonai is good," he had said.

Aden nodded. "This land is more than a promise fulfilled, it is a testimony of Yahweh's everlasting covenant, a haven more long-lasting than even my abba's old clay jar."

"Yahweh be praised," echoed their son, Baruch, the first to be born in Babylon.

"Yahweh be praised," Odelia said now, remembering. Her husband reached for her, and she squeezed his wrinkled hand. "Do you think, my husband, you may have one more adventure in those old legs of yours?"

He raised an eyebrow. "Oh, I think this old goat can manage one more adventure if it means his bride is beside him."

She laughed. "I would like to once more travel to Bethel, to the place where Adonai appeared to me."

Once they had settled in Babylon, she discovered a fascination with maps. It had not taken her long to surmise that she had traveled several miles north of Mizpah that horrible day. That placed her at Bethel, the very place her forefather Jacob had seen his stairway to the heavens. It was not lost on her that in her great distress, Adonai had met her there. She longed for it once more before she left this earthly life.

A knowing lit Aden's eyes. "If you truly wish to go, my wife, I will see if Jonathan will take us." Jonathan was their grandson, Baruch's son. "But what if you don't find that which you seek? What if Adonai chose to appear to you only then, when you needed Him most?"

She sniffed. "You are probably right. It's only that all these years, I have longed to see the man in the white robe again. He surely was a Great High Priest."

"I have an inkling you and I will both see him again very soon." Aden winked at her. "Do you still wish to go?"

Odelia looked around at her large family doing the work Jeremiah had started long ago. Building and planting. The time for new beginnings had finally come.

Adonai had guaranteed their future. A future marked not solely by survival but by Yahweh's grace. By His ability to bring life out of death.

"I suppose in a very meaningful way, He is here among us now, renewing this land as He renews our hearts." She placed her other hand atop her husband's so that his fingers were clasped between her palms. "For Adonai has never been contained to a single place, has He, my love?"

"'They will all know me, from the least of them to the greatest,'" he quoted.

"'For I will forgive their wickedness and will remember their sins no more,'" Odelia finished.

They sat for the rest of the day beneath the shade of an olive tree, savoring their family and what Yahweh was building through them.

Not only by their hands but through their hearts, Adonai be praised.

FROM THE AUTHOR

Dear Reader,

When I first learned of the opportunity to write about the mystery of the ark of the covenant, I was immediately excited. Truthfully, the whereabouts of the ark was not something I had dwelled on much, but as I threw myself into the many speculations surrounding the possible location of the historical treasure, I became more and more excited.

One likelihood I came upon was that the ark was smuggled out of Jerusalem by means of underground tunnels before the Babylonians broke through its walls and burned the temple. This, of course, got my writer's mind whirling! I tried to imagine how I could build a heroine around this story, and that was when Odelia was born.

For what if the priest, Pashhur, who had punished the prophet Jeremiah years earlier, had a daughter who sympathized not with her father but with the mistreated "weeping" prophet? What if she held special knowledge of the underground tunnels and was asked to aid in spiriting the ark out of the soon-to-be besieged city?

As I dived into the Old Testament, and focused heavily on the book of Jeremiah, I learned so much, both historically and spiritually. How often are we like those in ancient Jerusalem who affirmed the written Scriptures but rejected it in practice? Or perhaps we pick and choose what parts of God's Word we deem most important, while ignoring other matters He deems important. These are all themes I tried to weave into this story.

Another unsung biblical person I wanted to pay homage to was Baruch, Jeremiah's disciple and secretary. Baruch, son of Neriah, came from a family of high standing in the royal circle, and yet he chose to align himself, again and again, with Jeremiah and the things of God. Often, this made him an outcast among his contemporaries. His faithfulness reminded me that there is honor in quiet, humble, even thankless service to the Lord. He is *El Roi*, the God Who Sees.

Baruch (along with his fictional adopted son, Aden, in this story) places the things of God above their own personal ambitions. We have a precious part of the Lord's Word because of this man. No doubt he never imagined how long-lasting the part he played in this story would be, and yet he longed to be faithful to Yahweh, to seek first His kingdom.

May the same be said of you and of me. I pray this story blessed you as it did me as I wrote it. While I had never spent much time in the book of Jeremiah, my research has given me an entirely new appreciation for the message contained in this portion of Scripture. If nothing else, I pray this story will spur you to study it, and the entirety of God's Word, deeper. I pray you glimpse the majesty of His love and grace throughout the entirety of His Word.

May the Lord bless you and keep you; may He make His face shine upon you and be gracious to you; may He turn His face toward you and give you peace (Numbers 6:24–26).

With hope,
Heidi Chiavaroli

KEEPING THE FAITH

1. Odelia struggles between loyalty to her family and loyalty to what she believes the Lord is calling her to do. Have you ever felt pulled between the approval of people and the approval of God? How did you handle it, and what would you have done differently, if anything?
2. The temple was sacred ground for God's people, and yet Jeremiah hints at a new covenant where God would put His Law in the minds of His people and write it on their hearts. How did Jesus play a part in ushering in this new kingdom? What did He do on earth that announced this? How did His death and resurrection play a part in this as well?
3. The temple was good and of the Lord. And yet God was not pleased with how His people placed their allegiance to it over Him. What good things in your life have you placed above the Lord? How do we discern and measure our hearts so that the things of most importance would take precedence in our hearts and lives?
4. Aden tells Odelia, "It is not the size of our faith that is of import. It is Who we are placing our faith in that matters. Adonai is the faithful one." How do these words meet your spirit? How can they help you when you struggle with doubts or a weakened faith?

THE ARK OF THE COVENANT: A JOURNEY THROUGH HISTORY, FAITH, AND IMAGINATION

By Reverend Jane Willan MS, MDiv

Few artifacts have captured the imagination quite like the ark of the covenant. This legendary golden chest, described in vivid detail in the Hebrew Bible, stands at the crossroads of history, theology, and popular culture. Its disappearance over two and a half millennia ago has spawned a multitude of theories, inspired countless quests, and continues to fascinate scholars, believers, and adventure enthusiasts alike.

According to biblical accounts, the ark of the covenant was no ordinary relic. Crafted during the Israelites' exodus from Egypt, this ornate chest was said to house the stone tablets of the Ten Commandments, Aaron's rod, and a jar of manna. More than just a container for sacred objects, the ark represented the very presence of God among His people.

Imagine a wooden box, roughly four feet long and two-and-a-half-feet wide, overlaid with pure gold. On its lid sat two golden cherubim with outstretched wings, forming the "mercy seat" where God's presence was believed to dwell. This was more than a religious symbol; it was a powerful talisman that the Israelites carried into battle, believing it could part rivers, topple city walls, and strike down enemies.

For centuries, the ark played a central role in Israelite worship. It found its permanent home in the Holy of Holies within Solomon's Temple in Jerusalem. However, its fate after the Babylonian conquest of Jerusalem in 586 BC remains one of history's most enduring mysteries.

One hypothesis suggests that the ark found its way to Egypt before Jerusalem fell to the Babylonians. Proponents of this theory argue that priests or leaders, foreseeing the impending doom of Judah, took preemptive action to safeguard their most sacred relic.

This theory isn't as far-fetched as it might seem. Throughout biblical history, Egypt often served as a refuge for Israelites during times of crisis. Some researchers point to the Jewish colony on Elephantine Island in Egypt, where a temple existed in ancient times, as a possible hiding place for the ark.

However, like many theories surrounding the ark, concrete evidence remains elusive. The Egyptian escape theory relies on circumstantial arguments and historical reconstruction, making it an interesting but unproven possibility.

A more straightforward explanation for the ark's disappearance is the Babylonian destruction theory. This hypothesis claims that the ark was either destroyed or lost during Nebuchadnezzar II's conquest of Jerusalem in 586 BC.

This theory aligns with the biblical account of the temple's destruction and the detailed inventory of items taken as spoils by the Babylonians, which notably does not mention the ark. Critics argue that such a significant artifact would likely have been mentioned in Babylonian records if it had been captured or destroyed, leaving room for doubt about this explanation.

A more convincing theory suggests that the ark of the covenant was secretly hidden beneath the Temple Mount in Jerusalem before the Babylonian invasion. This hypothesis is rooted in both historical accounts and religious traditions.

King Solomon, anticipating future threats to the temple, constructed a complex network of tunnels and chambers beneath the Temple Mount specifically to safeguard sacred objects. Proponents of this theory argue that priests or temple guardians could have used these hidden passages to conceal the ark in a secure location, protecting it from desecration or theft.

In 1952, archaeologists made a remarkable discovery in Qumran Cave #3 near the Dead Sea: the Copper Scroll. Unlike other Dead Sea Scrolls written on parchment, this unique artifact was inscribed on copper, hinting at the importance of its contents. The scroll contains a list of sixty-four locations where various treasures are purportedly hidden, fueling speculation about the ark's whereabouts.

Some scholars have interpreted this ancient document as a potential map leading to the ark's secret location. They argue that the cryptic nature of the Copper Scroll's descriptions could be intentional, designed to protect the location of sacred artifacts from unauthorized discovery.

However, the scroll's content and purpose remain subjects of intense scholarly debate. While some view it as a genuine treasure map, others see it as a work of fiction or a symbolic text. The Copper Scroll continues to intrigue researchers and fuel the imagination of those searching for the lost ark.

The ark of the covenant's disappearance marks a pivotal moment in Judeo-Christian theology, coinciding with a significant shift in religious understanding. This transformation is perhaps best exemplified by the teachings of the prophet Jeremiah.

In Jeremiah 3:16, the prophet declares, "In those days, when your numbers have increased greatly in the land," declares the LORD, "people will no longer say, 'The ark of the covenant of the LORD.' It will never enter their minds or be remembered; it will not be missed, nor will another one be made."

This proclamation represents a radical departure from previous religious thought. Jeremiah's words suggest that the physical presence of the ark would no longer be necessary for the people to access or commune with God. This teaching marked a transition from a faith centered on tangible religious objects to one focused on spiritual connection and ethical living.

The loss of the ark, coupled with the destruction of the First Temple and the subsequent exile, forced a reevaluation of how to maintain faith without the central symbols and structures of the Israelites' religion. This led to an increased emphasis on prayer, study of sacred texts, and the performance of mitzvot, or commandments, as ways to connect with God.

In contemporary Jewish thought, the absence of the ark is often viewed as an opportunity for spiritual growth. It encourages believers to seek God's presence in everyday life rather than in a specific physical location or object. This shift aligns with the concept of the "portability" of faith, which became crucial during periods of displacement and persecution.

For Christianity, the transition away from the physical ark aligns with the New Testament teaching that Christ fulfills and supersedes the role of the ark. In this theological perspective, Jesus is seen as the ultimate meeting place between God and humanity, rendering the physical ark obsolete.

This evolution in religious understanding—from reliance on physical symbols to emphasis on spiritual connection—has had lasting impacts on both faiths. It has fostered a more internalized and personal approach to spirituality, where the divine presence is understood to be accessible through prayer, study, and righteous living rather than through physical artifacts or specific locations.

Historically, the ark's importance cannot be overstated. As a central element in the narratives of the exodus from Egypt, the conquest of Canaan, and the early monarchy period of Israel, the ark serves as a crucial touchstone for understanding the religious and political development of ancient Israel. Its presence or absence in various biblical accounts provides valuable context for historians studying the chronology and cultural dynamics of the ancient Near East.

In the field of archaeology, the search for the ark has spurred numerous expeditions and studies. While the ark itself remains elusive, these archaeological endeavors have contributed significantly to our understanding of ancient Israelite culture and religious practices. Excavations at sites mentioned in connection with the ark, such as Shiloh and Jerusalem, have yielded valuable insights into the historical periods in which the ark played a central role.

The mystery surrounding the ark of the covenant has made it a favorite subject in popular media, influencing literature, film, and wider popular culture. Perhaps the most famous portrayal is in the 1981 film *Raiders of the Lost Ark*, part of the Indiana Jones franchise. This depiction introduced the ark to a global audience, establishing its place in popular imagination as an object of supernatural power and inspiring adventure.

In literature, the ark has been the subject of numerous works of fiction and speculative nonfiction. Authors have woven tales of its discovery or have used it as a plot device in historical thrillers and religious mysteries. Television documentaries and series exploring the possible locations and fate of the ark have also become popular, often combining historical analysis with elements of treasure hunting.

Whether hidden in an Egyptian temple, destroyed by Babylonian invaders, or secreted away beneath Jerusalem, the ark's true fate remains shrouded in mystery. This uncertainty has only served to enhance its allure, inspiring generations of scholars, believers, and adventure seekers. The ark of the covenant stands as a powerful symbol of humanity's quest for meaning, our connection to the divine, and our enduring fascination with the mysteries of our shared past. As we continue to search for answers, the ark reminds us that some questions are valuable not just for their solutions but for the journey of discovery they inspire.

Fiction Author

HEIDI CHIAVAROLI

Heidi Chiavaroli (pronounced shev-uh-ROE-lee...sort of like *Chevrolet* and *ravioli* mushed together!) wrote her first story in third grade, titled *I'd Cross the Desert for Milk*. It wasn't until years later that she revisited writing, using her two small boys' nap times to pursue what she thought at the time was a foolish dream. Despite a long road to publication, she hasn't stopped writing since!

Heidi writes women's fiction, combining her love of history and literature to write both time-slip stories and contemporary fiction. She is a two-time Carol Award winner and a Christy Award finalist, a *Romantic Times* Top Pick, and a *Booklist* Top Ten Romance Debut. Heidi makes her home in Massachusetts with her husband, two sons, and Wyatt, her standard poodle.

Nonfiction Author

REVEREND JANE WILLAN, MS, MDiv

Reverend Jane Willan writes contemporary women's fiction, mystery novels, church newsletters, and a weekly sermon.

Jane loves to set her novels amid church life. She believes that ecclesiology, liturgy, and church lady drama make for twisty plots and quirky characters. When not working at the church or creating new adventures for her characters, Jane relaxes at her favorite local bookstore, enjoying coffee and a variety of carbohydrates with frosting. Otherwise, you might catch her binge-watching a streaming series or hiking through the Connecticut woods with her husband and rescue dog, Ollie.

Jane earned a Bachelor of Arts degree from Hiram College, majoring in Religion and History, a Master of Science degree from Boston University, and a Master of Divinity from Vanderbilt University.

Read on for a sneak peek of another exciting story in the Mysteries & Wonders of the Bible series!

TREACHEROUS WATERS:
Zahla's Story

by Melanie Dobson

Thunder roared through the valley and rippled across the sandy path. Zahla hugged her great-grandson to her chest, curling to protect his tiny body from the oncoming storm.

Merin had been born less than a month ago, during the plagues that Yahweh wrought across Egypt after their ruler refused to release the Israelites from slavery. Even though Zahla was nearing her ninety-sixth year, even though their walk out of Egypt had been long, she wouldn't let a drop of rain or blast of wind harm this little one. Like an egret shielding its chicks, she'd do anything to protect her family.

The ground shook again, stirring up dust that choked the refugees. While she'd never felt the earth quake, she'd heard many stories of old. The earth had shaken under Yahweh's hand when He brought their world into existence. Shaken when the God of Abraham destroyed the cities of Sodom and Gomorrah.

But what was Yahweh doing now?

Rain would refill their waterskins and cool their skin, but their tents wouldn't shelter them from lightning or the hailstones that had plagued Egypt.

Fellow Israelites pressed around Zahla as they rushed out of their tents and into a valley as if they could escape the storm. The Hebrew people, along with the others who'd fled Egypt with them, had set up camp below a ridge. Rumors filtered through the crowd about a body of water blocking their journey at the opposite end of the valley. A sea impossible to cross.

Then again, many rumors accompanied their walk out of Egypt. Though her eyesight remained strong, she couldn't see beyond the backs of her people or around the bend in the path. If there was indeed a sea before them, how could they escape the storm? The Israelites would never turn back toward Egypt.

Merin began to cry, but the noise was drowned in a different kind of sea. The flocks of goats and cattle bleating. The braying of donkeys. Children calling for their *imma* or *abba*. The shuffling and stomping of feet, crushing the sand as the rumbling grew behind them.

Zahla squinted as she searched for the beacon of cloud that had guided them away from Egypt, but it was hidden by dust. And in the midst of the confusion this evening, the threat of a storm, Zahla had lost sight of her oldest son and his children.

Her extended family numbered in the hundreds with the many cousins and children of her nieces and nephew. Only one of her sons had survived the harsh Egyptian taskmasters, and she'd left Egypt two weeks ago with Asher and his family. Asher's wife had passed on five years past, but he had three children and almost twenty grandchildren who had accompanied them on this journey.

Until Moses led the Hebrew people away from Egypt, the spacious vineyard in Goshen had been her home, but now home was a cluster of tents among more than a million refugees and their livestock, a number impossible for her to comprehend. Still, she wasn't worried. She always found her way back in the evening hours, content knowing that all her family was together in this wilderness. Far from Pharaoh's enslavement.

While Asher had faltered in his faith over the years, her son still fled with the refugees from Egypt, choosing Yahweh's promise of freedom over the oppression of Pharaoh's dark gods. Her grandchildren would see the miracles of Yahweh and the freedom prophesied long ago. The smallest ones like Merin wouldn't even remember the bondage, but she wanted all of them to forget the past now and embrace what Yahweh had ahead for them.

Zahla didn't see her family nearby, but at the edge of a pond, among the reeds, stood a girl about five or six years old. Tears trickled down the girl's thin cheeks, and Zahla felt her fear and loneliness as if it were her own. She crept toward the child, scanning the reeds for crocodiles or snakes. With the thunder, the crowds of people, any reptile would surely be scared back into the water, but Zahla had spent a lifetime searching among reeds for the monsters who waited near the shoreline to snatch a little one. No matter how many years she aged, she'd never stop her vigilance in protecting children.

With Merin and his tears secured in one arm, she reached out her free hand, wrinkled and worn, and placed it gently on the girl's shoulder. She didn't want to shout, but her voice had to rise above the clamor. "Did you lose your parents?"

The girl nodded.

"Merin and I will help you find them," Zahla said, nodding at the baby in her arms. "What is your name?"

"Sivian."

"A lovely name."

Sivian gazed across the crowd as though she was searching for her family as well. While they couldn't see the hills behind them, the thundering hadn't ceased. "What is that sound?"

Zahla was always honest, even with children. "I don't know."

Even though she wasn't certain about the noise, she'd begun to fear the rumbling was bringing unwelcome visitors instead of rain. That Pharaoh might have changed his mind once again and was still refusing to let Yahweh's people go.

"I happen to be an expert at finding families," Zahla told the girl.

Sivian nodded at the baby in Zahla's arm. "What is troubling him?"

"He misses his imma, I think."

"I understand," Sivian replied before reaching out for Zahla's free hand, with flocks of people rushing by as they moved toward the bend.

One of Zahla's family members would find them soon, before darkness set upon them, and then Asher would help her search for Sivian's parents.

As the crowd flowed through the valley, the thunder began to quiet, and Merin quieted as well. They would gather for news or direction from Moses tonight and wait for the fire. The pillar, she prayed, would turn again into a magnificent tower as it had every other night since they'd begun their desert journey. A flaming monument to their living God.

The pillar was one of many wonders in the past weeks. Fierce signs they'd seen in Egypt to demonstrate the power of Yahweh after He'd seemed silent for hundreds of years. Yahweh had rarely been silent with her, but now His voice—His power—was unmistakable to every man and woman in Egypt.

Their oppressors had suffered greatly when Pharaoh refused to let the people of Yahweh follow Moses into the wilderness, but Pharaoh, that cruel and stubborn man who believed himself a god, was intent on keeping the Hebrew people enslaved. His pride blinded him and his people.

Pharaoh had refused for weeks to free the Israelites, but after the heart-wrenching loss of his son, he relented. The Israelites, along with a handful of defiant Egyptians and slaves from other lands, had spent the weeks since then wandering between hills and through the Egyptian dry lands.

In the daylight hours, her people followed a white pillar that gleamed in the sun. At night, the cloud cylinder was replaced by a flame shooting into the heavens. When the pillar stopped, they set up camp and waited until the cloud began moving again. Then they would step forward with the promise of a new land ahead.

She didn't know when their caravan would finally settle. Even Moses, it was whispered, didn't know where the cloud would lead them next, but they couldn't continue down this path if a sea lay before them. They would have to go back.

Squinting, Zahla searched again for the pillar. Yahweh, she was certain, wouldn't abandon them. Not after all He'd done to free them from the oppression of Egypt.

Voices rumbled around her. People were worried. Distraught. Afraid for themselves and their families. If only they could stop for a moment—breathe—in what should be a quiet, reverent place.

"He's brought us out here to die," a woman nearby complained, and Zahla wished she could cover Sivian's ears.

"We are not going to die tonight," Zahla said, but the woman paid no heed as she continued her rant against Moses.

Even though more than fifty years had passed, the older members of their community remembered well the day that Moses, a Hebrew boy who'd become an Egyptian prince by adoption, had killed one of their taskmasters. At the time, many whispered that they were glad someone had finally confronted the whips, the cruelty, but with the death of an Egyptian came more labor for the men and more deaths among the Israelites. And much hatred for the Hebrew-Egyptian prince.

The Israelites feared and respected Moses alike. Mixed emotions impossible to untangle in the events of the past month. Moses and Aaron clearly operated under another power beyond their own, and while Zahla believed they heard the voice of Yahweh, some people thought the brothers were listening to a different god.

As the echoes of thunder calmed, the curtain of dust began to peel back. No rain clouds dotted the expanse, no sign of an impending storm. Instead, a wreath of pink and orange appeared as the sun prepared its descent on the western horizon. The white pillar of cloud slashed like a sword through the color, preparing to blaze a new path.

Sivian tugged on her tunic, and Zahla leaned down.

"I'm scared," the girl said, her pale brown eyes heavy with fear.

"We will find your parents."

"I know."

As the color flashed around them, Merin squirmed in her arms. "Then what are you afraid of?"

"Yahweh."

"Him you must fear." Zahla paused to comfort Merin. "But the Lord would not have brought us out here to abandon us."

Unless, the nagging voice teased inside her.

Unless Yahweh was so angry with the Israelites that He wanted to be rid of them all. She'd heard the stories of old about Yahweh cleansing and renewing their wicked world with a flood. He had promised, in the many colors of a rainbow, that He would never destroy the earth again, but what about His people?

Sivian dug her sandal into the sand. "He killed the others."

Zahla couldn't lean far, but she caught Sivian's gaze in hers. "Who did He kill?"

"The boys in Egypt," Sivian said.

"Ah…" Zahla's chest twisted at the memory. She wanted no child to die, Hebrew or Egyptian, and she didn't believe that Yahweh, the giver of life, wanted to kill either. But an angel of death had taken the lives of Egypt's firstborn sons when Pharaoh refused once again to free the Israelites.

"I do not understand the ways of Yahweh except He created life," Zahla said, "and He wants to free us from slavery. He wants freedom for everyone who follows Him."

And He seemed to want justice for those who'd persecuted her people for hundreds of years.

Merin returned to sleep as if he no longer had to be afraid, and her arm ached with his weight. If only she could sit in her chair back in Goshen and gently rock him as he slept. Or rest on a blanket or under the covering of their tent.

But more than rest, she wanted an end to the oppression for her children and their families. To live in a community separate from the gods of Egypt. A place where they belonged and a peaceful future for her descendants.

How her heart longed for peace.

No matter how tired her feet and her arms, she couldn't stop walking now.

"Look at that!" Zahla exclaimed as the crowd flowed around her and Sivian. The rumors, she realized, were true. The water ahead glowed red from the sun on their backs. It was too wide for swimming and probably too deep for wading.

They'd reached the end of this path.

"What is it?" the girl asked.

"A sea," Zahla said as a gust of salt-soaked air swept over them. They wouldn't be able to drink from this reservoir.

Sivian stretched up on her toes in attempt to see it, and Zahla wished she could pick her up.

"How will we cross it?" Sivian asked.

"It's not possible to cross," she said. "We will have to turn back into the valley."

Wander again in the wilderness.

Merin stirred in her arms, and Zahla gently bounced him. If only she had the strength of her youth. She could carry him all night if she must. But though her mind was still strong, her body failed her.

"Egyptians!" a man shouted behind her.

Zahla's feet dragged in the sand as she turned, Sivian clinging to her side. And she saw the source of thunder along the hillside. Chariots, hundreds of them, were clustered together on the rocks above them, ready to roll into the valley with their swords and might. Like a crocodile waiting for night so it could feast.

The Egyptians had already lost so much by Yahweh's hand. Why must they continue to torment her people?

Pharaoh must have changed his mind again in his fury, refusing to let another God defeat him.

With no weapons to defend themselves, the Israelites were trapped between Pharaoh's warriors and the Red Sea. Between their enemy of old and a new one blocking them from freedom. They were easy prey for those who had enslaved and now wanted to slaughter them.

Zahla's gaze rose to the billowy wings that sprouted from the pillar overhead, gleaming gold as the sun neared the horizon. Despite her confident words for Sivian, her own heart faltered.

Why had Yahweh led them here?

A NOTE FROM THE EDITORS

We hope you enjoyed another exciting volume in the Mysteries & Wonders of the Bible series, published by Guideposts. For over seventy-five years, Guideposts, a nonprofit organization, has been driven by a vision of a world filled with hope. We aspire to be the voice of a trusted friend, a friend who makes you feel more hopeful and connected.

By making a purchase from Guideposts, you join our community in touching millions of lives, inspiring them to believe that all things are possible through faith, hope, and prayer. Your continued support allows us to provide uplifting resources to those in need. Whether through our communities, websites, apps, or publications, we inspire our audiences, bring them together, and comfort, uplift, entertain, and guide them. Visit us at guideposts.org to learn more.

We would love to hear from you. Write us at Guideposts, P.O. Box 5815, Harlan, Iowa 51593 or call us at (800) 932-2145. Did you love *Covenant of the Heart: Odelia's Story*? Leave a review for this product on guideposts.org/shop. Your feedback helps others in our community find relevant products.

Find inspiration, find faith, find Guideposts.

Shop our best sellers and favorites at
guideposts.org/shop

Or scan the QR code to go directly to our Shop.

If you enjoyed Mysteries & Wonders of the Bible, check out our other Guideposts biblical fiction series! Visit https://www.shopguideposts.org/fiction-books/biblical-fiction.html for more information.

EXTRAORDINARY WOMEN OF THE BIBLE

There are many women in Scripture who do extraordinary things. Women whose lives and actions were pivotal in shaping their world as well as the world we know today. In each volume of Guideposts' Extraordinary Women of the Bible series, you'll meet these well-known women and learn their deepest thoughts, fears, joys, and secrets. Read their stories and discover the unexplored truths in their journeys of faith as they follow the paths God laid out for them.

Highly Favored: Mary's Story
Sins as Scarlet: Rahab's Story
A Harvest of Grace: Ruth and Naomi's Story
At His Feet: Mary Magdalene's Story
Tender Mercies: Elizabeth's Story
Woman of Redemption: Bathsheba's Story
Jewel of Persia: Esther's Story
A Heart Restored: Michal's Story

MYSTERIES & WONDERS of the BIBLE

Beauty's Surrender: Sarah's Story
The Woman Warrior: Deborah's Story
The God Who Sees: Hagar's Story
The First Daughter: Eve's Story
The Ones Jesus Loved: Mary and Martha's Story
The Beginning of Wisdom: Bilqis's Story
The Shadow's Song: Mahlah and No'ah's Story
Days of Awe: Euodia and Syntyche's Story
Beloved Bride: Rachel's Story
A Promise Fulfilled: Hannah's Story

ORDINARY WOMEN OF THE BIBLE

From generation to generation and every walk of life, God seeks out women to do His will. Scripture offers us but fleeting, tantalizing glimpses into the lives of a number of everyday women in Bible times—many of whom are not even named in its pages. In each volume of Guideposts' Ordinary Women of the Bible series, you'll meet one of these unsung, ordinary women face-to-face, and see how God used her to change the course of history.

A Mother's Sacrifice: Jochebed's Story
The Healer's Touch: Tikva's Story
The Ark Builder's Wife: Zarah's Story
An Unlikely Witness: Joanna's Story
The Last Drop of Oil: Adaliah's Story
A Perilous Journey: Phoebe's Story
Pursued by a King: Abigail's Story
An Eternal Love: Tabitha's Story
Rich Beyond Measure: Zlata's Story
The Life Giver: Shiphrah's Story
No Stone Cast: Eliyanah's Story
Her Source of Strength: Raya's Story
Missionary of Hope: Priscilla's Story

Befitting Royalty: Lydia's Story
The Prophet's Songbird: Atarah's Story
Daughter of Light: Charilene's Story
The Reluctant Rival: Leah's Story
The Elder Sister: Miriam's Story
Where He Leads Me: Zipporah's Story
The Dream Weaver's Bride: Asenath's Story
Alone at the Well: Photine's Story
Raised for a Purpose: Talia's Story
Mother of Kings: Zemirah's Story
The Dearly Beloved: Apphia's Story

Interested in other series by Guideposts?
Check out one of our mystery series!
Visit https://www.shopguideposts.org/fiction-books/
mystery-fiction.html for more information.

SECRETS FROM GRANDMA'S ATTIC

Life is recorded not only in decades or years, but in events and memories that form the fabric of our being. Follow Tracy Doyle, Amy Allen, and Robin Davisson, the granddaughters of the recently deceased centenarian, Pearl Allen, as they explore the treasures found in the attic of Grandma Pearl's Victorian home, nestled near the banks of the Mississippi in Canton, Missouri. Not only do Pearl's descendants uncover a long-buried mystery at every attic exploration, they also discover their grandmother's legacy of deep, abiding faith, which has shaped and guided their family through the years. These uncovered Secrets from Grandma's Attic reveal stories of faith, redemption, and second chances that capture your heart long after you turn the last page.

History Lost and Found
The Art of Deception
Testament to a Patriot
Buttoned Up

Pearl of Great Price
Hidden Riches
Movers and Shakers
The Eye of the Cat
Refined by Fire
The Prince and the Popper
Something Shady
Duel Threat
A Royal Tea
The Heart of a Hero
Fractured Beauty
A Shadowy Past
In Its Time
Nothing Gold Can Stay
The Cameo Clue
Veiled Intentions
Turn Back the Dial
A Marathon of Kindness
A Thief in the Night
Coming Home

SAVANNAH SECRETS

Welcome to Savannah, Georgia, a picture-perfect Southern city known for its manicured parks, moss-covered oaks, and antebellum architecture. Walk down one of the cobblestone streets, and you'll come upon Magnolia Investigations. It is here where two friends have joined forces to unravel some of Savannah's deepest secrets. Tag along as clues are exposed, red herrings discarded, and thrilling surprises revealed. Find inspiration in the special bond between Meredith Bellefontaine and Julia Foley. Cheer the friends on as they listen to their hearts and rely on their faith to solve each new case that comes their way.

The Hidden Gate
A Fallen Petal
Double Trouble
Whispering Bells
Where Time Stood Still
The Weight of Years
Willful Transgressions
Season's Meetings
Southern Fried Secrets
The Greatest of These

Patterns of Deception
The Waving Girl
Beneath a Dragon Moon
Garden Variety Crimes
Meant for Good
A Bone to Pick
Honeybees & Legacies
True Grits
Sapphire Secret
Jingle Bell Heist
Buried Secrets
A Puzzle of Pearls
Facing the Facts
Resurrecting Trouble
Forever and a Day

Find more inspiring stories in these best-loved Guideposts fiction series!

Mysteries of Lancaster County
Follow the Classen sisters as they unravel clues and uncover hidden secrets in Mysteries of Lancaster County. As you get to know these women and their friends, you'll see how God brings each of them together for a fresh start in life.

Secrets of Wayfarers Inn
Retired schoolteachers find themselves owners of an old warehouse-turned-inn that is filled with hidden passages, buried secrets, and stunning surprises that will set them on a course to puzzling mysteries from the Underground Railroad.

Tearoom Mysteries Series
Mix one stately Victorian home, a charming lakeside town in Maine, and two adventurous cousins with a passion for tea and hospitality. Add a large scoop of intriguing mystery, and sprinkle generously with faith, family, and friends, and you have the recipe for Tearoom Mysteries.

Ordinary Women of the Bible
Richly imagined stories—based on facts from the Bible—have all the plot twists and suspense of a great mystery, while bringing you fascinating insights on what it was like to be a woman living in the ancient world.

To learn more about these books, visit Guideposts.org/Shop